T0247439

THE
POWER
of
YOUR
WORDS
DEVOTIONAL

THE
POWER
of
YOUR
WORDS
DEVOTIONAL

60 Days of Declaring God's Truths

E. W. KENYON *and*
DON GOSSETT

WHITAKER
HOUSE

Unless otherwise indicated, all Scripture quotations are taken from the *New King James Version*®, © 1982 by Thomas Nelson. Used by permission. All rights reserved. Scripture quotations marked (KJV) are taken from the King James Version of the Holy Bible. Scripture quotations marked (NRSV) are taken from *The New Revised Standard Version Bible*, © 1989 Division of Christian Education of the National Council of the Churches of Christ in the USA. Used by permission. All rights reserved.

Boldface type in the Scripture quotations indicates the authors' emphasis.

The Power of Your Words Devotional
60 Days of Declaring God's Truths

Don Gossett Ministries
P.O. Box 2
Blaine, WA 98231
www.dongossett.com

Kenyon's Gospel Publishing Society
P.O. Box 973
Lynnwood, WA 98046-0973
www.kenyons.org

ISBN: 979-8-88769-287-6
eBook ISBN: 978-1-64123-675-1
Printed in the United States of America
© 2021 by Debra Gossett and Kenyon's Gospel Publishing Society

Whitaker House
1030 Hunt Valley Circle
New Kensington, PA 15068
www.whitakerhouse.com

Library of Congress Control Number for hardcover edition: https://lccn.loc.gov/2021942697

No part of this book may be reproduced or transmitted in any form or by any means, electronic or mechanical—including photocopying, recording, or by any information storage and retrieval system—without permission in writing from the publisher. Please direct your inquiries to permissionseditor@whitakerhouse.com.

1 2 3 4 5 6 7 8 9 10 11 ᴡ 31 30 29 28 27 26 25 24

CONTENTS

PART III:
ALIGNING YOUR WORDS WITH THE TRUTH

PART IV: LIVING WITH BOLD FAITH

INTRODUCTION

Christianity is often called the *great confession*. All things that are ours in Christ—salvation, healing, deliverance—are contingent upon the confession we make of Jesus's lordship and upon our affirmation of the truths in His Word. As the apostle Paul wrote to Timothy, *"You were also called and have confessed the good confession in the presence of many witnesses"* (1 Timothy 6:12).

This devotional is based on the writings of E. W. Kenyon and Don Gossett, whose primary message to believers was the power of their words. Kenyon would say we are what we confess, while Gossett would point out that our words can work wonders or blunders. In this sixty-day devotional, you will encounter many of their insightful teachings and also put them into practice by speaking aloud the Word and making personalized confessions based on what the Scriptures say.

Each entry features an accompanying prayer, a thought for personal reflection and application, and a set of daily readings from the Old and New Testaments. The entries are organized into four distinct sections, with a corresponding confession to be made as you begin that day's study.

+ Part I, "The Infallible, All-Powerful Word," contains devotions that hinge on the confession, "Though heaven and earth will pass away, God's Word stands forever," based on Matthew 24:35 and Isaiah 40:8.

+ Part II, "Confessing God's Word," introduces the practice of declaring God's Word, with the corresponding confession, "I am saved, for I confess the Lord Jesus with my mouth and believe in my heart that God has raised Him from the dead," based on Romans 10:9.

+ Part III, "Aligning Your Words with the Truth," reinforces the idea that our confessions must echo and affirm the Word of God. The confession in this section, from Matthew 19:26, is: "With God, anything is possible."

+ Part IV, "Living with Bold Faith," equips you to launch forth into a life of faith-fueled exploits, with the confession, "Christ lives in me, and I live by faith in Him who loved me and gave Himself for me," based on Galatians 2:20.

Whenever we study the Word of God, we should also pray and ask God for wisdom and a receptive heart. The Holy Spirit is our teacher, and we must rely on Him to illuminate the Word and give us insight and understanding.

You can discover the power of your words when it is God's Word on your lips. Begin today living a life powered by words of truth!

PART I

THE INFALLIBLE, ALL-POWERFUL WORD

*"Though heaven and earth will pass away,
God's Word stands forever."*
See Matthew 24:35; Isaiah 40:8.

DAY 1

GOD'S CONFESSION

The more we read the Bible, the clearer it becomes that the Word of God is His confession. From Genesis to Revelation, the Scriptures provide us with a continual confession of God's greatness, His ability, His love, and His great heart as our loving Father. And it is up to us to echo His confessions by declaring our belief in them.

For example, if we attest to the truth of Psalm 34:10—*"Those who seek the LORD shall not lack any good thing"*—and if we stand by our confession, then God will make good all that we have confessed.

If we dare to confess Philippians 4:19—*"My God shall supply all [my] need according to His riches in glory by Christ Jesus"*—our heart grows strong and our faith surges.

God is obligated to stand by and care for His own. He cannot fail us. Just consider the wonder of these declarations He has made:

No weapon formed against you shall prosper, and every tongue which rises against you in judgment you shall condemn. This is the heritage of the servants of the LORD, and their righteousness is from Me. (Isaiah 54:17)

Fear not, for I am with you; be not dismayed, for I am your God. I will strengthen you, yes, I will help you, I will uphold you with My righteous right hand. (Isaiah 41:10)

Because of such Scriptures, we can say with the psalmist, "*The* LORD *is on my side; I will not fear. What can man do to me?*" (Psalm 118:6). God is our Protector and Caretaker, just as He was for the Israelites. Do you recall what happened to Pharaoh and Egypt, and the Philistines? (See Exodus 14:21–31; 1 Samuel 14.) Do you remember what happened to all the nations that laid their hands upon Israel while they were keeping the covenant? "*He permitted no man to do them wrong; yes, He rebuked kings for their sakes, saying, 'Do not touch My anointed ones, and do My prophets no harm'*" (1 Chronicles 16:21–22).

God will take care of us in the same way He took care of the Israelites, for He watches over His Word to perform it for all of His children. (See Jeremiah 1:12.)

Prayer: Almighty God, I praise You for the record we have of Your great confessions about Yourself and about us, Your children. Help me to trust in what You have said and done. In Jesus's name, amen.

Thought: Are there any confessions God has made that you have struggled to accept or believe? What will it take for you to believe them?

Readings: Jeremiah 1:12–19; Hebrews 3:1–6

DAY 2

CHRIST'S CONFESSION

In the four Gospels, we see Jesus continually making confessions about who He was and why He had come to earth.

For starters, He called Himself the Good Shepherd: *"I am the good shepherd. The good shepherd gives His life for the sheep"* (John 10:11).

He also called Himself the Light of the World: *"I am the light of the world. He who follows Me shall not walk in darkness, but have the light of life"* (John 8:12).

Here are some other tremendous confessions of our Lord Jesus Christ:

I am the way, the truth, and the life. (John 14:6)

I am the resurrection and the life. He who believes in Me, though he may die, he shall live. (John 11:25)

I am the bread of life. He who comes to Me shall never hunger, and he who believes in Me shall never thirst. (John 6:35)

My Father, who has given them [those who follow Christ] *to Me, is greater than all; and no one is able to snatch them out of My Father's hand.* (John 10:29)

Jesus's confession ultimately led Him to Calvary: *"Therefore the Jews sought all the more to kill Him, because He not only broke the Sabbath, but also said that God was His Father, making Himself equal with God"* (John 5:18).

It was there on the cross atop Calvary that Jesus bought our freedom. And, in the words of Jesus, *"if the Son makes you free, you shall be free indeed"* (John 8:36). This freedom stems from our knowledge and confession of the truth, for *"you shall know the truth, and the truth shall make you free"* (John 8:32). We declare that whom the Son has made free is free in reality, that sin cannot lord it over us any longer. *"For sin shall not have dominion over you, for you are not under law but under grace"* (Romans 6:14).

We confess disease and sickness cannot keep us in bondage because we understand the power of Jesus's words on our lips. He told us that those who believe *"will lay hands on the sick, and they will recover"* (Mark 16:18). He gave us the blessed assurance that *"whatever you ask in My name, that I will do, that the Father may be glorified in the Son"* (John 14:13).

The Word on our lips not only makes us free but sets others free. The Word on our lips heals the sick. The Word on our lips creates faith in the hearts of those who hear us. The Word on our lips will change the lives of others as they listen. It is the very life of God in those words—the life Jesus purchased for our sake by His death and resurrection.

> *Prayer:* Heavenly Father, I love the words of Jesus. They are life to me, and I declare them and their implications for me, day in and day out. Thank You for Your Son and His faithful confession of Your Word—an example I commit to follow. In Jesus's name, amen.
>
> *Thought:* Are your spoken words fostering faith in those who hear you?
>
> *Readings:* Isaiah 9:1–3; John 6:63–64

DAY 3

CHRIST'S CLAIMS
TO DEITY

Let's take a look now at the confessions Jesus Christ made of His deity—His oneness with God the Father. The following are ten claims Jesus made in the gospel of John, every one of which illustrates His divine nature. It is because of the reality of these claims that we can find salvation, redemption, and power in Jesus's name.

Read these Scriptures carefully. You may wish to locate them in your Bible and underline or highlight them for future reference.

1. *"Most assuredly, I say to you, the Son can do nothing of Himself, but what He sees the Father do; for whatever He does, the Son also does in like manner. For the Father loves the Son, and shows Him all things that He Himself does; and He will show Him greater works than these, that you may marvel"* (John 5:19–20).

2. *"I have come in My Father's name"* (John 5:43).

3. *"For if you believed Moses, you would believe Me"* (John 5:46).

4. *"I am the bread of life. He who comes to Me shall never hunger, and he who believes in Me shall never thirst"* (John 6:35).

5. "*Most assuredly, I say to you, he who believes in Me has everlasting life....I am the living bread which came down from heaven. If anyone eats of this bread, he will live forever*" (John 6:47, 51).

6. "*You both know Me, and you know where I am from; and I have not come of Myself, but He who sent Me is true, whom you do not know. But I know Him, for I am from Him, and He sent Me*" (John 7:28–29).

7. "*He who sent Me is with Me. The Father has not left me alone, for I always do those things that please Him*" (John 8:29).

8. "*I have come that they may have life, and that they may have it more abundantly*" (John 10:10).

9. "*I and My Father are one*" (John 10:30).

10. "*I am the resurrection and the life. He who believes in Me, though he may die, he shall live*" (John 11:25).

Do we dare to confess what we are and what we have in Christ? Do we dare to confess John 1:16: "*Of His fullness we have all received, and grace for grace*"? We have received Christ's fullness, but it does us no good unless we translate it into a confession. We need to confess that what He has said is true, and then we need to demonstrate our belief by the way we live.

Make this your continual confession: "God is my Father; I am His child. As a son or daughter in His family, I am taking my place. I am acting my part. I am in Christ, and Christ is in me." Your heavenly Father will be to you what you confess Him to be.

Prayer: Lord God, I rejoice in confessing that You are my Father and I am Your child. I rejoice in the implications of Your Son Jesus's being one with You. Thank You for sending Him to win me to You. I will live and speak as Your child from this day forward. In Jesus's name, amen.

Thought: Which one of the ten confessions of Jesus that we shared here seemed the most astounding to you?

Readings: Psalm 121; John 17:10–12

DAY 4

ECHOING JESUS'S AFFIRMATIONS ABOUT HIMSELF

Have you ever considered the astounding number of statements Jesus said about Himself? One of them was this astonishingly bold claim: *"I am the way, the truth, and the life. No one comes to the Father except through Me"* (John 14:6).

Prayer is our way of getting to the Father. Under the first covenant, only the high priest could gain access to God's presence—and that only once a year, through the holy of holies. But now, Jesus has proclaimed, "I am the new way into My Father's presence, and if you will take Me to be your Savior and receive eternal life, then you can come through Me into My Father's presence anytime you wish."

The veil that had long hidden the holy of holies from the eyes of the people has been torn in two. Now, anyone who follows Jesus can approach God's throne.

Jesus said, "I am the Water of Life. He that drinks of the water that I give will never thirst." (See John 4:14.) We who have tasted of this living water know that it is true—we will never thirst again. We don't go to the wells of psychology, philosophy, or sense knowledge and reasoning to quench our parched souls because we have a better drink that truly satisfies.

Jesus also said of Himself, *"I am the light of the world. He who follows Me shall not walk in darkness, but have the light of life"* (John

8:12). "Light" also means "wisdom," and Jesus has become our wisdom. He is our light to dispel the darkness of life's problems. We don't walk in the darkness of sense knowledge any longer. We may occasionally lapse and descend into the valley of sense knowledge, but when we turn to God's eternal Word, we again find our *"light of life,"* our Savior.

When our hearts are yearning for nourishment, Jesus is there to satisfy us. He told us, *"I am the bread of life. He who comes to Me shall never hunger"* (John 6:35). The food of this world may sustain us for a while, but it is not enough. Jesus said, *"Man shall not live by bread alone, but by every word that proceeds from the mouth of God"* (Matthew 4:4).

Those who learn to feed on the Word of God will leave a legacy such as Job, who said, *"I have treasured the words of His mouth more than necessary food"* (Job 23:12), and Jeremiah, who said, *"Your words were found, and I ate them"* (Jeremiah 15:16). Like them, we must feed on this Bread of Life, the Word of God.

Jesus is the solution to the human spirit problem. He answers every cry of our broken spirits. Jesus is the answer to life's enigma. He is the Light of life's problems. He is all that our hearts could ever ask to know. He satisfies the hungry and the thirsty.

In John 6:47, Jesus said, *"He who believes in Me has everlasting life."* Put another way, Jesus is letting us know that if we believe in Him, we receive Him and thus receive eternal life, the nature of God. Jesus's words mean everything to us as believers.

Prayer: Father God, thank You for making a way through Jesus for me to enter into Your presence through prayer, that I might drink and never thirst, eat and never hunger. I acknowledge Your Son Jesus as the light of my life and will seek His wisdom on all matters. In Jesus's name, amen.

Thought: Have you tasted of the water that truly satisfies?

Readings: Psalm 23; John 6:26–40

DAY 5

THE NAME ABOVE
ALL NAMES

Jesus has given us the legal right to use His name to speak to the Father. He has given us His power of attorney. Using the beautiful name of Jesus is the most powerful way to speak that's available to us as Christians. It is not superstition or mysticism to speak and act in the wonderful, glorious, omnipotent name of Jesus.

> *Whatever you do in word or deed, do all in the name of the Lord Jesus, giving thanks to God the Father through Him.*
> (Colossians 3:17)

Jesus gave to all believers the right to speak in His name. When He said that He would do anything that His disciples asked in His name (see John 14:13–14), the term "ask" implies "commanding in the name of Jesus" that diseases, demons, and adverse circumstances depart! When we "ask" by praying to the Father in the all-powerful name of Jesus, He answers our prayers.

> *Most assuredly, I say to you, whatever you ask the Father in My name He will give you....Ask, and you will receive, that your joy may be full.* (John 16:23–24)

Jesus is the name above all other names (see Philippians 2:9), the name at which *"every knee should bow, of those in heaven, and of those on earth, and of those under the earth, and that every tongue should confess that Jesus Christ is Lord, to the glory of God the Father"* (verses 10–11). His name is a strong tower to which the righteous can run and find safety. (See Proverbs 18:10.)

As often as you can, speak in the name of Jesus. Right now, try saying His name three times: "Jesus! Jesus! Jesus!" Don't you feel God's love enfolding you?

While ministering at open-air evangelistic events in several cities in India, Don faced thousands of people each night. Over and over, he invoked the name of Jesus as he commanded diseases to depart from people. In the city of Nagercoil, seventy-seven notable miracles were recorded. Similar results were witnessed in Trivandrum. Just as all those people did, you too can receive healing through Jesus's name. You can be like the man to whom Peter and John ministered healing in Acts 3, of whom Peter said that "[Jesus's] *name, through faith in His name, has made this man strong, whom you see and know. Yes, the faith which comes through Him has given him this perfect soundness in the presence of you all*" (verse 16).

Also in India, Don had the immense joy of leading tens of thousands of people to a saving faith in Jesus Christ. As these multitudes came to believe in the death, burial, and resurrection of Jesus Christ and confessed Him as their Lord and Savior, they received everlasting life. You, too, can be saved right now, by simply believing with your heart and confessing with your tongue. "*Whoever calls on the name of the LORD shall be saved*" (Joel 2:32).

Call on the name of Jesus today. Whoever believes in Him and trusts in His name will never be put to shame! (See Romans 10:11; Psalm 25:3.)

Prayer: Heavenly Father, I praise and thank You for giving me the right to call on and pray in the almighty name of Jesus. Help me to make a regular habit of praying and acting in His name. In Jesus's name, amen.

Thought: What have you noticed as you have prayed in and called on the name of Jesus?

Readings: Psalm 25; Romans 10:9–13

DAY 6

THE AGELESSNESS OF GOD'S WORD

The name "Jehovah" means "I am the one who is" or simply "I Am"—past, present, and future. There is also three tenses in redemption: what Jesus did and who He was on earth; what Jesus is and what He is doing now; and what Jesus will be and shall do. Both Jesus and His Father are eternal and unchanging. Accordingly, the Scriptures say, *"Jesus Christ is the same yesterday, today, and forever"* (Hebrews 13:8).

The Word God spoke in the past is also now. His Word is alive! It has just as much authority today as it did when He first spoke it. His Word has the same power to save and the same power to heal.

Exodus 16:18–20 relates the story of the Israelites receiving a daily dose of food called manna as they lived in the desert, awaiting their entry into the Promised Land. The manna had to be gathered every morning and could not be saved for the following day. If anyone tried to save up the manna, it became unfit to eat. So it is with the Word: It must be ingested daily, studied daily, and meditated on daily, or else it loses its power in our lives.

The Israelites had no way of preserving the manna for future consumption, whether by dehydrating, canning, or any other means. That source of food was good for only one day. How striking a thought that is! Your experiences in Christ are very similar. The experience of yesterday is of little value now. Many of us have tried to preserve our spiritual experiences, but it simply can't be done. Jesus is a "now" Jesus. What He said must always be experienced anew, at this moment. It is what He is doing now, what He is now, that counts.

When Jesus said, "*Whatever you ask the Father in My name He will give you*" (John 16:23), that truth was to last until He returned to earth again. When He said, "*In My name…they will lay hands on the sick, and they will recover*" (Mark 16:17–18), that promise was to remain valid until His second coming. The Word is as fresh as though it had been spoken yesterday.

When Jesus said, "*If two of you agree on earth concerning anything that they ask, it will be done for them by My Father in heaven*" (Matthew 18:19), that truth is just as new and fresh as if He had uttered it this very morning. The assurance recorded in John 15:7, "*If you abide in Me, and My words abide in you, you will ask what you desire, and it shall be done for you*," is just valid as though He had said it an hour ago.

No Word from God ever grows old. It has perennial vigor. It renews itself continually.

Prayer: Father God, I thank You for the timelessness of Your promises. Help me to take You at Your Word, just as Jesus's disciples did when they heard Him speak. In Jesus's name, amen.

Thought: Are there any aspects of God's Word that you have considered to be "expired" or no longer valid? How does today's meditation alter your thinking?

Readings: Isaiah 40:3–8; 1 Peter 1:3–5

DAY 7

THE WORD OF GOD AS OUR INHERITANCE

When we fully realize that the Father is one with His Word, the Bible becomes a brand-new book for us. When we read and hear the Scriptures as the words of the Master, speaking directly to us, then His Word becomes a reality for us.

Nowhere do we see Jesus claiming to be an original or taking credit for the origin of His words. Rather, He always declares that the words He is speaking come directly from His Father. Consider this telling passage:

> [Jesus said,] *"If anyone hears My words and does not believe, I do not judge him; for I did not come to judge the world but to save the world. He who rejects Me, and does not receive My words, has that which judges him—the word that I have spoken will judge him in the last day. For I have not spoken on My own authority; but the Father who sent Me gave Me a command, what I should say and what I should speak."*
> (John 12:47–49)

When Jesus healed the sick, He did so by the Word of the Father on His lips. When He stood outside the tomb of His recently deceased friend and called, *"Lazarus, come forth!"* (John 11:43), it was the Father's words that worked the miraculous act of raising Lazarus from the dead.

When Jesus spoke to a fig tree that subsequently withered and died, it was the Father's Word upon His lips that caused the event. (See Mark 11:12–14, 20–24.)

When He hushed the sea, saying, *"Peace, be still!"* (Mark 4:39), it was the Father's Word on His lips. (See also Matthew 8:26; Luke 8:24.) When He multiplied the bread and the fish, healed the sick, and raised the dead, it was the Father's Word upon His lips that did the work. (See Matthew 14:19–21; Mark 5:21–43.)

When Jesus said, *"I am the light of the world"* (John 8:12), He was only speaking that which His Father gave Him to speak.

Thus, the Father's words on Jesus's lips brought life to the dead, healing to the sick, perfect limbs to the maimed, food to the hungry, sight to the blind, and deliverance from the fear of a watery grave to the disciples.

Can you grasp the significance of all this? Jesus did all these things with words—the words His Father gave Him to speak. And He has given those very words to us! Jesus Christ is the surety of the new covenant, from the gospel of Matthew to Revelation, and we can use His words today and every day. His words on our lips will perform the same kind of miracles that the Father's words performed when spoken by His lips.

We have the words that bring healing, salvation, deliverance, joy, peace, and rest. We have the words that will build faith into the discouraged, strength into the weak, hope into the hopeless, and deliverance for those who are being held in bondage. God's ability is wrapped up in His words, which were spoken by Jesus and must be spoken by us today.

Prayer: Father God, I praise You for giving me the right to use Your Word, just as Jesus did, for the working of miracles and deliverance. Make me a faithful steward of Your wonderful Word. In Jesus's name, amen.

Thought: How has today's entry altered the way you view the Word of God?

Readings: Isaiah 55:1–3; John 5:17–30

DAY 8

"YOU ARE OF GOD"

John was speaking to all believers throughout all time when he said, "*You are of God, little children, and have overcome them* [the spirits of this world], *because He who is in you is greater than he who is in the world*" (1 John 4:4). You, dear believer, are "*of God*." There are others who belong to a different class—those who "*are of the world. Therefore they speak as of the world, and the world hears them*" (1 John 4:5).

But *you* are of God, born from above, born of water and the Spirit; therefore, you have entered the kingdom of God. (See John 3:3, 5.)

You have received God's nature, life, and ability. With His nature, you receive the characteristics of God. If you fellowship with Him, you acquire the habits of God that were demonstrated by Jesus during His earthly walk.

"*You are of God, little children, and have overcome them*" (1 John 4:4). What an expression of victory! The work has been accomplished. When Jesus overcame the adversary, you were with Him. His victory was your victory. And now He calls you an overcomer.

How do you overcome the adversary? We find our answer in 1 John 2:14, where the apostle says, "*I have written to you, young men, because you are strong, and **the word of God abides in you**, and you have overcome the wicked one.*" Those young men to whom John was writing overcame in their present-day combat through the Word that was living in them.

The Word is God's voice, God speaking to us. It is a part of Himself. It is God in us who has overcome the evil one. The forces that were arrayed against us were brought into subjection, into captivity.

We read in Revelation 12:11, "*They overcame him* [the devil] *by the blood of the Lamb and by the word of their testimony.*" You are a conqueror because of your testimony. It is your testimony, your confession of faith, which defeats the devil. You win when you confess that the same Spirit that raised Jesus from the dead now dwells in you and is healing your body, keeping your mind clear and sound, and making you a victor in all circumstances.

Remember, "*He who is in you is greater than he who is in the world*" (1 John 4:4). I like to think that the Holy Spirit did not lay aside any of His ability, wisdom, or might when He made his dwelling in the believer's body. He can use the sword of the Spirit through your lips and thereby conquer your every foe.

Prayer: Lord God, I confess that I am in You, and You are in me. Your Holy Spirit indwells my heart and makes me an overcomer in all circumstances. All praise and glory to You for the victory, Lord! In Jesus's name, amen.

Thought: Have you ever really reflected on the fact that you share in Jesus's victory over death and the devil?

Readings: Psalm 16; 1 Corinthians 15:56–57

DAY 9

CONFIDENCE ROOTED IN GOD'S WORD

As we launch into a life of bold faith, learning to confess God's Word in every situation, we need to see exactly why we have the right to make these confessions.

We know that we have the right to boldly confess God's Word because of Hebrews 13:5–6: "*He Himself has said, 'I will never leave you nor forsake you.' So we may boldly say: 'The* Lord *is my helper; I will not fear. What can man do to me?'*" It is because of what "*He Himself,*" our heavenly Father, has said that "*we may boldly say.*"

Because God has said, "*I am the* Lord *who heals you*" (Exodus 15:26), we may boldly say, "Yes, Lord, I am in health because You are the Lord who heals me."

Because God has said, "*Whosoever offers praise glorifies Me*" (Psalm 50:23), we may boldly say, "I am glorifying my Creator by offering praise and worship to Him."

Because God has said of His own Word, "*I am the* Lord*. I speak, and the word which I speak will come to pass…I will say the word and perform it*" (Ezekiel 12:25), we can count on God's Word being good. It cannot fail because God cannot fail.

Along the same lines, the Lord has said:

So shall My word be that goes forth from My mouth; it shall not return to Me void, but it shall accomplish what I please,

and it shall prosper in the thing for which I sent it.
                                                                 (Isaiah 55:11)

Because of this assurance, we can boldly place and proclaim our confidence in God's Word. We confess that God is Lord of our lives, and that He is Lord over disease, sickness, and Satan. We hold fast to our confession of Jesus's absolute lordship over everything that would keep us in bondage or hinder us from partaking of the finished work of Christ. In the face of every need, we confess, "The Lord is my Shepherd; I shall not want for anything." (See Psalm 23:1.)

If we dare to confess healing on the grounds of the Word, then there is no sickness for us. God's Word will heal us if we continually confess it. Our bodies will respond to our minds and will obey our confession. Psalm 107:20 says, *"He sent His word and healed them, and delivered them from their destructions."* Jesus was that Word. Now the name of Jesus and the words of Jesus have become our healing.

Confession is a way of affirming the Word of God. It is a confession of our confidence in what God has spoken, and it is an essential practice if God's Word is to become our reality.

Prayer: Heavenly Father, I confess my confidence in Your Word. Thank You that I can trust You to fulfill Your promises and make good on Your every word. May I hold fast to my confession all the days of my life. In Jesus's name, amen.

Thought: How would you rate your current level of confidence in God's Word?

Readings: Isaiah 55:10–13; Matthew 4:1–11

DAY 10

CONFIDENCE FOR DIVINE DELIVERANCE

W e can have absolute trust in the promises God makes in His Word, including those He has made regarding His intention to fight for us and deliver us from the enemy of our souls.

Because He has said, *"I have come that they may have life, and that they may have it more abundantly"* (John 10:10), we may boldly say, "I have that abundant life in me right now because I have received Jesus Christ as my Lord and Savior."

Because His Word says, *"If God is for us, who can be against us?"* (Romans 8:31), we may boldly say, "God is for me, and no one can succeed against me."

Because He has said, *"Whoever confesses Me before men, him I will also confess before My Father who is in heaven"* (Matthew 10:32), we may boldly say, "Jesus is confessing me right now before the Father because I am confessing Him before men."

Because He has said, *"When the enemy comes in like a flood, the Spirit of the Lord will lift up a standard against him"* (Isaiah 59:19), we may boldly say, "God's Spirit is raising a standard of defense on my behalf at the very same time the enemy is heaping pressure on me; praise the Lord, my case is His!"

Because He has said, *"The Lord is near to all who call upon Him, to all who call upon Him in truth"* (Psalm 145:18), we may boldly say, "The Lord is near me now because I call upon Him in truth."

Because He has said, *"The LORD will fight for you, and you shall hold your peace"* (Exodus 14:14), we may boldly say, "I know that God is fighting for me because I am holding my peace; I have committed this battle into His hands."

Because His Word says, *"Thanks be to God who always leads us in triumph in Christ"* (2 Corinthians 2:14), and *"In all these things we are more than conquerors through Him who loved us"* (Romans 8:37), we may boldly say, "I am more than a conqueror through Christ who loves me."

Because His Word says, *"No good thing will He withhold from those who walk uprightly"* (Psalm 84:11), we may boldly say, "The Lord withholds no good thing from me, including protection and deliverance, because I am walking uprightly before Him."

Because His Word says, *"[Cast] all your care upon Him, for He cares for you"* (1 Peter 5:7), we may boldly say, "I am free of care because all my cares have been cast upon the Lord."

Because He has said, *"The one who comes to Me I will be no means cast out"* (John 6:37), we may boldly say, "I have come to the Lord with my sins, burdens, and failures, and He has taken me in even so."

Because His Word says, *"Commit your way to the LORD, trust also in Him, and He shall bring it to pass"* (Psalm 37:5), we may boldly say, "The Lord is working out every detail of my life because I have committed all of it to Him, and I am fully trusting in Him."

Our deliverance is certain when we take God at His Word!

Prayer: Father God, I entrust every part of my life to You, trusting that You will work all things together for my good and delivering me from evil. Praise be to Your glorious name! In Jesus's name, amen.

Thought: In what areas are you trusting God for deliverance today?

Readings: Psalm 140; Romans 8:28

DAY 11

CONFIDENCE FOR SUPERNATURAL HEALING

The wonderful assurances in God's Word continue with promises of healing and perfect health.

Because His Word says, *"Beloved, I pray that you may prosper in all things and be in health, just as your soul prospers"* (3 John 1:2), we may boldly say, "I have a right to prosperity and health because I am prospering in my soul."

Because His Word says, *"He Himself took our infirmities and bore our sicknesses"* (Matthew 8:17), we may boldly say, "I am free from sickness and disease because Jesus Christ bore all my ailments for me."

Because His Word says, *"He who raised Christ from the dead will also give life to your mortal bodies through His Spirit who dwells in you"* (Romans 8:11), we may boldly say, "God is giving life to my mortal body now by the very same Spirit that raised Jesus from the dead. His Spirit dwells in me; thus, I am free from weakness and sickness."

Because He has said, *"These signs will follow those who believe: In My name…they will lay hands on the sick, and they will recover"* (Mark 16:17–18), we may boldly say, when laying hands on the sick, "They are recovering because I am believing in and acting on God's Word."

Because His Word says, *"You shall serve the LORD your God, and He will bless your bread and your water. And I will take sickness away from the midst of you*" (Exodus 23:25), we may boldly say, "Sickness is taken away from me, and my bread and water are blessed because I am serving the Lord my God."

Because He has said, "*To you who fear My name the Sun of Righteousness shall arise with healing in His wings*" (Malachi 4:2), we may boldly say, "The Lord is arising with healing for me now because I fear His name."

Because His Word says, "*He sent His word and healed them*" (Psalm 107:20), we may boldly say, "Healing is mine now; the Lord is healing me through His Word because I have received His Word into my heart."

Prayer: Father God, thank You for the blessed assurance that Jesus has borne my sickness and carried my disease. Give me faith for healing, for myself and others. In Jesus's name, amen.

Thought: Which of the Scriptures shared in today's entry encouraged you the most?

Readings: Isaiah 53; Luke 5:12–15

DAY 12

CONFIDENCE FOR
ANSWERED PRAYERS

Thanks be to God for the priceless gift of prayer—a means of communicating with Him and receiving comfort, wisdom, and guidance in return.

Because He has said, *"Before they call, I will answer; and while they are still speaking, I will hear"* (Isaiah 65:24), we may boldly say, "The Lord is answering my prayer even now as I pray. In fact, He was already working on the answer before I prayed!"

Because He has said, *"Call to Me, and I will answer you, and show you great and mighty things, which you do not know"* (Jeremiah 33:3), we may boldly say, "The Lord is answering me and showing me great and mighty things because I am calling to Him."

Because He has said, *"Whatever you ask in My name, that I will do, that the Father may be glorified in the Son"* (John 14:13), we may boldly say, "The Father is being glorified in the Son because Jesus is doing great things for me as I ask for them in His name."

Because His Word says, *"Delight yourself also in the LORD, and He shall give you the desires of your heart"* (Psalm 37:4), we may boldly say, "The Lord is granting me the desires of my heart because I am delighting myself in Him."

Because He has said, *"If you abide in Me, and My words abide in you, you will ask what you desire, and it shall be done for you"* (John

15:7), we may boldly say, "I am abiding in Christ, and He is living in me and answering my petitions."

Because He has said, *"Ask, and you will receive, that your joy may be full"* (John 16:24), we may boldly say, "My joy is full because I am asking and receiving in Jesus's name."

Because He has said, *"Whatever things you ask when you pray, believe that you receive them, and you will have them"* (Mark 11:24), we may boldly say, "I shall have what I have prayed for because I have prayed for it and I believe it is mine, even now."

Because He has said, *"Everyone who asks receives"* (Matthew 7:8), we may boldly say, "I know I am receiving because I have asked. 'Everyone' includes me—there are no exceptions."

Prayer: Lord, I thank You for the promise of answered prayers. I believe that You hear me when I call to You and that You will answer me in Your perfect timing. In Jesus's name, amen.

Thought: What are some specific prayers of yours that God has answered?

Readings: Jeremiah 29:11–14; Matthew 7:7–12

PART II

CONFESSING GOD'S WORD

*"I am saved, for I confess the Lord Jesus with
my mouth and believe in my heart that God has
raised Him from the dead."*
See Romans 10:9.

DAY 13

CONFESSION PRECEDES POSSESSION

John 3:16 proclaims a wonderful truth: *"God so loved the world that He gave His only begotten Son, that whoever believes in Him should not perish but have everlasting life."* God the Father gave His Son Jesus to the world, to those who were perishing. He gave Jesus to the men who crucified Him, the men who made a crown of thorns to press upon His brow, the men who nailed Him to the cross. Strange, isn't it?

This truth brings us face-to-face with a strange word that we don't find being used in the Old Testament the way it is used in the New Testament. That word is *grace*.

> *The law was given through Moses, but grace and truth came through Jesus Christ.* (John 1:17)

Grace is love at work: love giving and doing for the unlovely and unworthy.

Now, what does it mean to believe in Jesus? *Believe* is a verb, while *faith* is a noun. Believing is an action word; faith is the result of a person's having acted or believed. Believing, in the New Testament sense, means an action that results in possession.

Jesus provided us with the key when He said, *"He who believes in Me **has** everlasting life"* (John 6:47). In the mind of the Father, believing *is* possessing. And how do we gain possession? By acting on His Word. Believing, then, is acting on what the Father has spoken.

When you believe in Christ, it means you have taken possession of what the Father has given you. Jesus is yours—He is your Savior, Lord, and Light! The moment you take possession of Christ, you become a new creation who is *"born from above"* (John 3:3 NRSV).

Believing is an act of the will. It's a decision, a choice. It indicates a willingness to turn your back on your past life and start anew, translated out of the realm of death and sin into the realm of life and love, where you are a child of God. Believing means being ready to take possession of what God, in His great love, gave to you. It means saying, "Father, thank You for Jesus and for His gift of eternal life. Thank You for the remission of my sins, the wiping out of my past. Thank You that I am now a new creation. Thank You for choosing me in Christ before the foundation of the world and for enabling me to respond to that call."

You have a vast inheritance in Christ, but you must take possession of it. And there is no possession without confession. Again, believing is taking possession. It is simply acting on the Word of the Father—telling the world that you are in Christ and claiming Him as your Lord and Savior. It is shouting aloud that there is now no condemnation for you, for you are in Christ Jesus!

The possession does not come until you have made a joyful confession. When you make that confession, all becomes yours in reality, for realization follows confession. When you begin to act on the Word, the possession becomes a reality for you. At that point, you *cash in* on what grace has given you. It is never a question of faith or emotion; the essential thing is taking hold of what God has already given you, to acknowledge the gift, thank the Giver, and claim your rights as a child of God.

Prayer: Lord God, thank You for making me Your child and for granting me such rights as I can hardly speak of, they are so wonderful. I claim those rights now, acknowledging You before the world as my Lord and Savior and committing to continually confess and possess Your promises. In Jesus's name, amen.

Thought: Have you taken hold of what God has already given you?

Readings: Ezekiel 18:21–23; Ephesians 1:3–6

DAY 14

THE POWER OF
YOUR CONFESSION

Few Christian believers truly understand the importance of confession. We're not talking about confession strictly as admitting to wrongdoing, as many people think of it. Instead, what we are talking about is confessing what we believe, testifying to what we know. Our confession—our witness—ought to be a principal area of consideration as we live out our faith.

Our confession centers on four primary things: first, what God in Christ has done for us; second, what God through His Word and His Spirit has done for us; third, what we are to the Father in Christ; and, fourth, what God can do through us or what His Word can do when spoken by us.

You cannot confess or witness to things you do not know. It is what you know personally about the Lord Jesus Christ and about who you are in Him that counts. The following are some basic confessions we can make based on what God's Word says about us:

- "I am a brand-new creature because I am in Christ." (See 2 Corinthians 5:17.)

- "I am redeemed and forgiven of my sins by the blood of Jesus Christ." (See Ephesians 1:7.)

- "God is with me and will never leave me; He will strengthen me and uphold me with His righteous right hand." (See Isaiah 41:10.)

- "If God is for me, who can be against me?" (See Romans 8:31.)

- "I can do all things through Christ, who gives me the strength I need." (See Philippians 4:13.)

- "I will triumph over my enemies through Christ who gives me the victory." (See Psalm 44:5.)

Because of what the Bible says, you can rightly confess that Christ is your Savior, so you have a redemption that God planned and wrought in His Son. You are a new creation of which God alone is the Author and Finisher. You have a righteousness that allows you to stand in His presence as though your sin had never been. You not only have righteousness reckoned to you, but you also have righteousness imparted to you in the new nature that you received from Him. You have received His nature, His life; and in this life and nature is the life of God. This makes you righteous, even as He is righteous.

You can say with joy, *"Sin shall not have dominion over* [me]" (Romans 6:14). You can confess that whatever you ask of the Father in His name, you will have. (See John 14:13–14.)

Confession is faith's way of expressing itself. And faith, like love, is revealed only in action and word. (See James 2:20.) There is no faith without confession, and your confession determines how far your faith will grow. Confess daily what the Father is to you, what Jesus has done and is now doing for you at the right hand of the Father, and what the mighty Holy Spirit is doing for you—and you will build for yourself a positive, rock-solid faith life.

Prayer: Heavenly Father, thank You for the wonderful truths I find in Your Word. Fill me with faith that grows as I confess who You are, who I am in You, and what You have done and are now doing in and through me. Let me use my words to build myself a firm foundation of ever-deepening faith. In Jesus's name, amen.

Thought: What confessions are you making to reinforce your faith?

Readings: Isaiah 41:8–10; 2 Corinthians 5:17–19

DAY 15

SPEAK WHAT YOU BELIEVE

We invariably speak what we believe, whether it is right or wrong. Jesus said, *"Out of the abundance of the heart the mouth speaks"* (Matthew 12:34). When we are exercising the true spirit of faith, we believe the Word and we speak that Word.

For example, the Word says in Ephesians 1:7, *"In Him [Christ] we have redemption through His blood, the forgiveness of sins, according to the riches of His grace."* Accordingly, we speak something along these lines: "I am redeemed from the kingdom of darkness through the precious blood of Jesus."

The Word says in 1 John 2:25, *"This is the promise that He has promised us—eternal life."* Therefore, we say, "I have eternal life according to God's great promise."

The Word records Jesus as saying, in Matthew 28:20, *"I am with you always, even to the end of the age."* Thus, we speak with confidence, "The Lord is with me always, even until the very end of my earthly life's journey."

The Word says in Hebrews 11:16, *"God is not ashamed to be called their God, for He has prepared a city for them."* Therefore, we speak, "God is my God, and He has prepared a beautiful city for me."

The Word says in Proverbs 11:25, *"The generous soul will be made rich, and he who waters will also be watered himself."* Along the same lines, we say, "The Lord is prospering and watering my life. By His grace I am a generous and cheerful giver."

The Word says in Jude 1:24, *"Now to Him who is able to keep you from stumbling, and to present you faultless before the presence of His glory with exceeding joy."* Therefore, we say with full assurance, "The Lord can and will keep me from falling and will present me faultless before His presence."

Many believers dwell too much on their problems and don't push past them to make the proper confessions. A wrong confession affirms defeat, failure, and the supremacy of Satan. When you talk about your struggles with the devil and rehash how he has hindered you and sent you troubles, you are confessing defeat and using your words to glorify your adversary.

Most of the confessions we hear nowadays glorify the devil, destroy faith, and hold people in bondage. If you are to live in the victory Jesus Christ has won for you, then you must speak only faith and not doubt, always affirming that which the Word of God says. That's because the confession of your lips that has grown out of the faith in your heart will absolutely defeat the devil in every combat.

Prayer: Heavenly Father, thank You that I can have confidence in the truths and promises I find in Your Word. Help me to always speak in a way that aligns with Your Word. In Jesus's name, amen.

Thought: Do the words you speak align with what God's Word says?

Readings: Proverbs 11:9–12; 2 Corinthians 4:13

DAY 16

THE POWER OF GOD'S WORD ON YOUR LIPS

The apostle Paul wrote, "*If you confess with your mouth the Lord Jesus and believe in your heart that God has raised Him from the dead, you will be saved*" (Romans 10:9). The word "*saved*" here means "healed." It is your mouth that makes the confession of the faith that is in your heart or your spirit. When you make this confession, it means you have come to believe or know that the Word of God is absolute.

God says that He watches over His Word to see that it is performed, or carried out. (See Jeremiah 1:12.) What does the Word of God do for you? The Word of God saves you. The Word of God heals you. The Word of God supplies you with finances and resources. It is the Word that does all these things.

Psalm 107:20 says that God "*sent His Word and healed them.*" Jesus is that Word. His words were Himself.

When you make the Word of God your own word, and it dwells in you richly, then you can speak the Word and know that whatever you say is yours. You can say, "By His stripes, I am healed" and know that healing is yours. (See Isaiah 53:5.)

Your words are your confession—a confession that either confirms or denies the Word of God. Maintaining your confession of God's Word—holding fast to the Word of truth—is the secret of success and victory in the divine life.

You hold fast to your confession that God laid your sins upon Jesus, and that gives you eternal life.

You hold fast to your confession that you are healed by His stripes, and that gives you your healing.

You hold fast to your confession that *"in all these things we are more than conquerors through Him who loved us"* (Romans 8:37), and you are more than a conqueror.

You hold fast to your confession that *"my God shall supply all* [my] *need according to His riches in glory by Christ Jesus"* (Philippians 4:19), and your every need is supplied.

Can you see now that your faith is measured by your words, or your confession? Your confession is an expression of your estimation of the Word of God.

Prayer: Father God, I commit to holding fast to my confession of Your Word. What You have said, I will say. Help me to maintain a consistent affirmation of Your wonderful promises in the Scriptures. In Jesus's name, amen.

Thought: What confessions of the Word do you need to start making on a consistent basis?

Readings: Numbers 22:35–38; Hebrews 4:12

DAY 17

FIVE CONFESSIONS OF A FAITH-FILLED BELIEVER

The following are five key confessions that every faith-filled believer should be able to make.

1. THE LORDSHIP OF JESUS

If you confess with your mouth the Lord Jesus and believe in your heart that God has raised Him from the dead, you will be saved. For with the heart one believes unto righteousness, and with the mouth confession is made unto salvation.

(Romans 10:9–10)

When you can confess the absolute lordship of Jesus Christ, you can also confess the absolute righteousness that is imparted to you in your redemption. Dare to confess before the world and before the throne of God that Jesus is now your Lord and that you have received salvation and *"become the righteousness of God in Him"* (2 Corinthians 5:21). Confess that you are a new creation of which Jesus Christ is the Head and Lord. The Word has taken the place of Jesus in your life, and you are committed to obeying the Word as you would obey Jesus if He were standing before you.

2. THE SUFFICIENCY OF GOD TO SHOULDER YOUR BURDENS

First Peter 5:7 exhorts us to cast *"all your care upon [God], for He cares for you."* Confess to the world that you no longer carry any cares, anxieties, or burdens. You can never be unnerved and unfit for your life's work. Your mind is complete and clear. Your spirit is free. Your testimony has the anointing of the Holy Spirit upon it because He bears every burden, shoulders every load, and meets every need, according to His riches in glory by Christ Jesus. (See Philippians 4:19.)

3. THE FACT THAT BECAUSE OF GOD, YOU LACK NOTHING

Confess to the world Psalm 23:1: "*The LORD is my shepherd; I shall not want.*" You do not want for money. You do not lack health or rest. You are not failing in strength or health. You do not want for anything! Jesus alone is all you need. The all-sufficiency of Christ is a living reality for you. What a life is yours! What a sense of security, power, and victory! You are not afraid to believe that God shall do "*exceedingly abundantly above all that* [you] *ask or think, according to the power that works in* [you]" (Ephesians 3:20), to meet and even exceed your needs.

4. THE POWER OF GOD TO HEAL AND RESTORE

Surely He [Jesus] *has borne our griefs and carried our sorrows; yet we esteemed Him stricken, smitten by God, and afflicted. But He was wounded for our transgressions, He was bruised for our iniquities; the chastisement for our peace was upon Him, and by His stripes we are healed.* (Isaiah 53:4–5)

Boldly proclaim the truthfulness of these verses. Every disease, every weakness, and every infirmity has been laid on Jesus Christ, meaning that you are free of them forever. Just as Jesus bore your sin, He bore your disease. You stand complete in Him, free from the burden, the power, the pain, and the effects of disease. This confession gives you a healthy body, a sound mind, and a conquering spirit.

5. THE IMPLICATIONS OF YOUR POSITION IN CHRIST JESUS

Confess 1 Corinthians 1:30: *"You are in Christ Jesus, who became for us wisdom from God—and righteousness and sanctification and redemption."* Christ has been made all these things unto you. You do not need to pray for wisdom, because Christ is your wisdom. You need not ask for righteousness, because you have become the righteousness of God in Him. You don't have to ask Him to sanctify you—He *is* your sanctification! You need not pray for redemption; you are redeemed because He is your redemption! What a confession to make to the world!

> *Prayer:* Father God, I praise You for making Christ Jesus my righteousness, sanctification, and redemption. What unspeakable joy I have in believing Your promises and living in the light of them! Help me to make these confessions routinely and to build my life upon them. In Jesus's name, amen.
>
> *Thought:* How do these five confessions change your perspective on a situation you're facing right now?
>
> *Readings:* Psalm 23; 2 Corinthians 5:17–21

DAY 18

CONTINUALLY CONFESS YOUR REDEMPTION AND HEALING

It is crucial to make a continual confession of your redemption from Satan's dominion—an ongoing declaration that he no longer rules you with condemnation or fear of disease. You must hold fast to this confession, for your confession is Satan's defeat.

As a believer, you need not ask to be healed; you *have been* healed. You need not request to be made righteous; you *have already been* made righteous. You need not ask to be redeemed; your redemption is an absolute fact.

In the mind of your heavenly Father, you are perfectly healed and perfectly free from sin because He laid your diseases and sins upon His Son. His Son was made to be sin with your sins. He was made sick with your illnesses. In the mind of Christ, you are perfectly healed because He can remember when He was made sin with your sins, when He was made sick with your illnesses. He remembers when He put your sin and diseases away forever.

In the mind of the Holy Spirit, you are absolutely free from both sin and sickness, for He remembers when Christ was made sin and when He was made sick. He remembers when He raised Jesus from the dead.

Christ was free from your sin and your sickness. Both of those had been put away prior to His resurrection. And since *"by His stripes we are healed"* (Isaiah 53:5), we are already healed; we need only thank Him for the work He has already accomplished.

What you continually confess will either imprison you or set you free. A strong confession, coupled with a corresponding action on the Word, brings God on the scene. Holding fast to your confession even when your senses contradict it shows that you have become established in the Word.

Prayer: Lord God, I confess today and every day that Christ purchased my redemption from sin and sickness; therefore, I no longer live under the dominion of the devil but in the blessed kingdom of Your love and light. In Jesus's name, amen.

Thought: Do you have trouble maintaining a constant confession of your redemption and healing?

Readings: Isaiah 53; 1 Peter 2:21–25

DAY 19

AFFIRM YOUR IDENTITY IN CHRIST

Always declare the new creation, not the old. Say it with confidence: "I am a new creature in Christ Jesus; the old things have passed away, and all things have become new." (See 2 Corinthians 5:17.)

Continually speak your righteousness in Christ, never unworthiness. Affirm the following: "I am the righteousness of God in Christ Jesus." (See 2 Corinthians 5:21.)

Speak the language of the new kingdom of God's dear Son in which we now dwell, not the former kingdom of darkness from which we have been saved. Remember, God *has delivered us from the power of darkness and conveyed us into the kingdom of the Son of His love, in whom we have redemption through His blood, the forgiveness of sins* (Colossians 1:13–14).

Affirm that you are an heir of God and a joint heir with Christ Jesus, not your old identity as a captive to sin and slave of Satan. Testify: "I have a rich inheritance. I am blessed with every spiritual blessing. The Father Himself loves me." (See Ephesians 1:3; Romans 8:17.)

Confess that the Son has made you free (see John 8:36), and you will possess absolute freedom.

Confess that *"the righteous are bold as a lion"* (Proverbs 28:1), and you will exhibit lionhearted boldness in spiritual warfare.

Confess that you are a branch of the true, living Vine (see John 15:5), and you will possess fruitful life wherever you go.

Confess that you are *"the righteousness of God in* [Christ]" (2 Corinthians 5:21), and you will possess the ability to stand freely in God's holy presence, as well as victoriously in Satan's presence.

Confess that you are *"the temple of the living God"* (2 Corinthians 6:16), and you will experience the reality of God dwelling in you and walking with you.

Prayer: Heavenly Father, thank You for the wonderful promises in Your Word of life, health, and favor. Help me to cling to those promises and affirm only success, never failure. In Jesus's name, amen.

Thought: What negative thoughts have you given voice to recently? How can you turn those around with a life-affirming Word?

Readings: Psalm 139:14; Romans 8:9–17

DAY 20

CAST OFF YOUR INFERIORITY COMPLEX

For ages, the church has taught sin consciousness rather than righteousness consciousness. Believers have been taught that they are weak, sinful, and unworthy until they pray, "God, O God, have mercy on my poor soul."

This emphasis on our sinful nature is distinctly anti-Christ, and we did not realize it; it is anti-redemption, and no one took notice that when people become children of God, they have God's nature—God's very life—in them. That nature and that life give them a standing before the Father.

Was the apostle Paul not clear enough when he wrote, "*There is therefore now no condemnation to those who are in Christ Jesus, who do not walk according to the flesh, but according to the Spirit*" (Romans 8:1)? Was he vague when he cried out, "*Who shall bring a charge against God's elect? It is God who justifies*" (Romans 8:33)? God is the one who has declared you righteous and justified you.

Many preachers, pastors, and evangelists have done a grave injury to the cause of Christ, however unwittingly. Some of the sermons we consider the greatest or the most famous are those that put men and women under condemnation—those that propel them to the altar, sobbing and pleading for forgiveness—even though they have walked with God for many years. We should instead show them what they are in Christ.

We have thought that the confession of our sins was a proof of personal goodness, and so we have confessed our shortcomings and our failings again and again; every testimony we have made has been one of lack, want, or weakness. We have torn believers out of their rightful places in the family of God and have placed them among the regenerate. We have used God's message of reproof to Israel through the prophets against the church instead of lifting up the church and showing believers what they are in Christ so that they can be an overcoming body. We have burdened them with guilt and bitter criticism.

We have neglected to say, "*My God shall supply all* [my] *need*" (Philippians 4:19); "*I can do all things through Christ who strengthens me*" (Philippians 4:13); "*God is the strength of my heart*" (Psalm 73:26); and "*It is God who works in* [me] *both to will and to do for His good pleasure*" (Philippians 2:13).

God has made provision for us to live without condemnation. His redemption takes us out of Satan's dominion and the new birth removes the devil's nature from us.

The Bible says, "*Therefore, if anyone is in Christ, he is a new creation; old things have passed away; behold, all things have become new*" (2 Corinthians 5:17). We have a new nature and a new relationship with our heavenly Father. We are children of God. We stand complete in His completeness, and we are filled with His fullness. We are members of His very body.

We are the sons and daughters of God Almighty, having been recreated by God Himself, through His own Word. We stand in His completeness. Never be ruled by an inferiority complex that says otherwise.

Prayer: Heavenly Father, forgive me for times when I have confessed only my sin and not the truths about my nature as Your child. Replace my sin consciousness with a righteousness consciousness whereby I recognize and rejoice in the way You have saved, cleansed, and redeemed me. In Jesus's name, amen.

Thought: Have you developed an *inferiority complex* of sin consciousness that you need to replace with a righteousness consciousness that gives you confidence in your standing before the Lord?

Readings: Psalm 103:1–18; 1 John 3

DAY 21

NO CONDEMNING CONFESSIONS

Confession is made with the mouth, not only for the good things God has promised us, but also for sickness, defeat, bondage, lack, and failure.

Refuse to have a bad confession. Refuse to make negative confessions. Repudiate any dual confessions, such as when you say in one moment, *"By His stripes we are healed"* (Isaiah 53:5) and in the next moment, "But the pain is still there. I'm still dealing with symptoms."

Negative confessions really can produce negative results. Do not fall prey to the tendency to be *"snared by the words of your mouth"* (Proverbs 6:2).

It is of utmost importance that you look to God for help in overcoming any unruly speech habits, for your words can get you into serious trouble. Words spoken in the heat of the moment— words of anger, harshness, retaliation, bitterness, unkindness, and negativity—produce trouble for us.

Beloved, make the following Scriptures your prayer today and every day:

> Let the words of my mouth and the meditation of my heart be acceptable in Your sight, O LORD, my strength and my Redeemer. (Psalm 19:14)
>
> Set a guard, O LORD, over my mouth; keep watch over the door of my lips. (Psalm 141:3)

Progress to a higher level of living in the kingdom of God by believing and confessing that you are who God says you are. Think that way. Talk that way. Act that way. Train yourself to live on the level of what is written about you in God's Word.

Do not permit your thoughts, your words, or your actions to contradict what God has said about you.

Although you may not master the ability to make only positive confessions within a day, a week, or even a month, you will learn it and improve upon it as you continue to practice it faithfully. Because God has said it, we may boldly say the same thing!

Faith grows with confession. Every time you confess your righteousness in Christ, or God's righteousness in you, you begin to develop and grow. Every time you confess your faith, your faith grows. If you never confess, you'll never grow. Just as you feed love with words, you feed faith with words—your words and God's Word. If you speak unbelief, weakness, and failure, your spirit will descend to the level of those words. Your faith will weaken and become enfeebled. Your righteousness will be of no effect.

The measure of your faith will be the measure of your confession. Hold fast to your confession of faith, righteousness, and redemption, and you will have confidence that your needs, lacks, sins, and shortcomings will be swallowed up in your confession of the promises of God.

Prayer: Father God, I thank You for giving me the ability to grow my faith through my positive confessions of Your Word. Help me to make a practice of doing this and to silence all negative confessions, lest my faith decrease and my life be robbed of Your power. In Jesus's name, amen.

Thought: What negative confessions do you need to turn into positive, faith-filled confessions?

Readings: Psalm 19; James 3:8–12

DAY 22

CONSIDER IT DONE

The law of confession holds that you confess you have a thing *before* you consciously possess it. We can see this law at work, for example, in regard to one's entry into the household of faith. In his letter to the Romans, Paul laid out the law for entering into the household of faith:

> *If you confess with your mouth the Lord Jesus and believe in your heart that God has raised Him from the dead, you will be saved. For with the heart one believes unto righteousness, and with the mouth confession is made unto salvation.*
>
> (Romans 10:9–10)

You can see that it is with the heart that you believe Jesus is your righteousness, and it is with your lips that you make a confession of salvation. This confession of the lips comes *before* God acts upon your spirit and recreates it. You said, "Jesus died for my sins, according to the Scriptures, and I now acknowledge Him as my Lord." In the instant that you acknowledged Him as Lord and Savior, you received eternal life.

You cannot have eternal life until you've confessed that you have it. Your confession precedes God's taking action to recreate you.

The same is true in regard to healing. When you are sick, confess, "According to Isaiah 53:5, He has borne my sicknesses and carried my pains, and by His stripes, I am healed." Even if the disease and its symptoms do not leave your body at once, hold fast to your confession, being confident that God will make good on His

Word. You can know that you are healed because God said you are healed, regardless of any symptoms that may linger. Only when you boldly confess what you possess do you come to possess it.

Faith is governed by confession. Don't repudiate your healing by saying that you have been prayed for and are waiting for God to heal you. If you are sick and have been prayed for, your confession should be as follows: "The Word declares that I am healed, and I thank the Father and praise Him for it because it is a fact."

The same goes for your needs. We read in Philippians 4:6, *"In everything by prayer and supplication, **with thanksgiving**, let your requests be known to God."* Why must prayer be made with thanksgiving? Because your expression of gratitude shows that you know the thing is done. You've asked for it; now you have it and are thanking your heavenly Father for it.

Then, *"the peace of God, which surpasses all understanding, will guard your hearts and minds in Christ Jesus"* (Philippians 4:7). You need not worry any longer! You have that which you have asked for. You aren't going to get the money you need; you *already have it*. It is just as real as though it were in your pocket. You are not going to get your healing; you *already have it* because you have God's Word, and your heart is filled with rapture.

Prayer: Heavenly Father, forgive me for repudiating Your Word by doubting its efficacy and forgetting that what You have promised, You have done as I confess it to be so. Thank You for Your wonderful promises and blessings without number. In Jesus's name, amen.

Thought: What have you been *waiting on* from God that you should consider already done or given?

Readings: Isaiah 53:4–12; Philippians 4:4–7

DAY 23

WE BECOME WHAT WE THINK AND SPEAK

Criminals are not criminals by accident. They think themselves into wrongdoing and then act on their thoughts. They think about crime for so long that they lose the sense of its wrongness.

Every form of wrongdoing is the product of a sequence of wrong thinking. It may take years for a person to turn into a murderer, but it happens. It is the result of dreaming of doing something that, at first, seems shocking and horrifying but later becomes a familiar companion and the behavior that makes someone a criminal.

The same principle applies to every aspect of life. The great musician must live in a mental realm of music to be able to produce it. The artist must exist in the realm of renowned paintings, sculptures, and other works of art. If an artist is a painter, he first dreams his picture; next, he paints it with his imagination. A great architect mentally constructs a bridge years before she receives an order for that project. A great novelist is one who puts on paper that which he has dreamed. We become what we most intently think we are—and what we intently think we are, we tend to speak.

Love is largely the work of the spirit through one's imagination. For example, a man loves a woman and dreams of her until she becomes a part of his dream life, to the point that it becomes hard for him to live without her. A person may dream of wealth until, after a bit, his or her surroundings grow unpleasant, to the extent that he or she may be tempted to do almost anything that would secure for them the thing about which they have been dreaming.

That is why it is imperative to master your dream life by managing the thoughts you dwell on and the ones you give voice to. It is essential to govern your dreams and flights of imagination. You must put your dream machinery to work on the right kind of fabric. If your imagination must weave, make it weave the proper cloth. Bring it under control of the Holy Spirit, "*casting down... every high thing that exalts itself against the knowledge of God, bringing every thought into captivity to the obedience of Christ*" (2 Corinthians 10:5).

Out of your dreams will come either a masterful personality or a weak, vacillating one. If you want to succeed, you can; your career and your future will be molded out of the things you dream today. Someone is going to be the next great musician, artist, doctor, lawyer, architect, pastor...why should it not be you?

Almost all the truly great men and women carved their futures out of their dream lives, even while surrounded by poverty, lack of resources, and other types of hardship. This is the power of one's thought life and the resulting confession one makes.

> **Prayer:** Lord God, thank You for the dreams You have placed within me. Help me to rein them in and stay obedient to You and Your ways, even as I think about the future and make plans for my career and family. Whatever I do and whatever I say, may I bring glory to You. In Jesus's name, amen.
>
> **Thought:** Is your dream life submitted to the Holy Spirit?
>
> **Readings:** Proverbs 23:1–18; 2 Corinthians 10:1–6

DAY 24

THE DANGER OF
CANCELED CONFESSIONS

There is grave danger in dual confessions. You can't afford to contradict your testimony or believe one thing and say another. You can't confess the absolute faithfulness of God's Word—that the Lord is your Healer, Supplier, and Provider—and then turn around and confess your sickness, your weakness, your lack of finances, or another type of lack. Your confession of sickness, disease, and lack will destroy what you are in Christ and what He is to you. This is one of the most dangerous of all confessions.

We find multiple warnings about contradictory confessions in the book of James:

> If any of you lacks wisdom, let him ask of God, who gives to all liberally and without reproach, and it will be given to him. But let him ask in faith, with no doubting, for he who doubts is like a wave of the sea driven and tossed by the wind. For let not that man suppose that he will receive anything from the Lord; **he is a double-minded man, unstable in all his ways.**
>
> (James 1:5–8)
>
> Draw near to God and He will draw near to you. Cleanse your hands, you sinners; and **purify your hearts, you double-minded.** (James 4:8)

A man once asked E. W. to pray for his healing. After he did so, the man said, "I want you to keep on praying for me." What did he wish this man of God to pray for? He said, "For my healing, of course." He was told, "Prayer will be of no value. You have just denied the Word of God." By his confession, the man had annulled the prayer.

Jesus said, "Those who believe will lay hands on the sick, and they shall recover; and whatever you ask in My name, that will I do." (See Mark 16:18; John 14:13.)

Your confession must align with the Word. If you have prayed in Jesus's name, you are to hold fast your confession. It is all too easy to destroy the effect of your prayer by a negative confession.

> *Prayer:* Father, forgive me for the times when I have nullified Your Word with my confessions of fear and doubt. Help me to hold fast to my confession of Your truth. In Jesus's name, amen.
>
> *Thought:* What confessions have you made recently that don't align with God's Word?
>
> *Readings:* Genesis 18:12–15; James 3:1–12

PART III

ALIGNING YOUR WORDS WITH THE TRUTH

"With God, anything is possible."
See Matthew 19:26.

DAY 25

THE VALUE OF CONFESSING WITH INTENTIONALITY

We have already established that you will always walk in the light of your testimony, whatever it may be. If you confess something with your mouth, your confession reacts upon your heart or your spirit. The Word becomes real only as you confess its reality, for realization follows confession.

Satan fears your testimony, for he knows that if you confess what you are in Christ, you will act on your confession. If you confess your fears, those fears will rule you. If you confess the dominion of a disease, that illness will assert its lordship over your body even more fully.

But if you confess your freedom—declaring that the Son has made you free—God makes that confession your reality. If you realize that Jesus met defeat and conquered it, and you dare to confess as much, then defeat and failure lose their dominion over you.

Thinking faith thoughts and speaking faith words leads your heart out of defeat and into victory. When you confess God's Word and align your own words with it, God watches over His Word to make it good. (See Jeremiah 1:12.) Yet there is no action on the part of God without your confession.

Hebrews 4:14 says, "*Seeing then that we have a great High Priest who has passed through the heavens, Jesus the Son of God, let us hold fast our confession.*" What is the confession to which we are to hold fast? That in Him we have a perfect redemption.

The Father "*has delivered us from the power of darkness and conveyed us into the kingdom of the Son of His love, in whom we have redemption through His blood, the forgiveness of sins*" (Colossians 1:13–14). Few people seem to grasp the fact that their redemption does not become a reality until they confess it.

In the face of apparent defeat, confess your redemption and deliverance, and they will become a reality. Don't ask for redemption but thank God for it. Your redemption is not a promise but a fact.

> *Ye **know** that ye were not redeemed with corruptible things, as silver and gold…but with the precious blood of Christ, as of a lamb without blemish and without spot.*
>
> (1 Peter 1:18–19 KJV)

Your confession must be a confession of the absolute faithfulness of God's Word, His finished work, and the reality of your relationship as a son or daughter. Your words determine your faith. Your words are your confession.

If you continually confess lack, you believe in lack; your confession will surely become a reality. If you believe in failure and weakness, you will confess them, and you will live up to the standard of that confession. Make sure that you understand the value of making confessions with intentionality, for they will surely bear the corresponding fruit in your life.

Prayer: Father, forgive me for failing to realize the impact of my words and for anything I have spoken that has not aligned with Your Word. Help me to make positive, faith-filled confessions at all times. In Jesus's name, amen.

Thought: Have you been speaking with intentionality?

Readings: Jeremiah 1:4–10; Hebrews 4:11–16

DAY 26

AFFIRMATION MAKES ANYTHING POSSIBLE

Faith and unbelief are both built out of affirmations. The affirmation of a doubt builds unbelief, while the affirmation of faith builds strength to believe more and more. When you affirm that the Word of God cannot be broken, you affirm that the Word and God are one, and that when you trust in the Word, you are also trusting in God the Father.

Abraham trusted in the Word when he counted that God was able to make good on His promises, as unlikely as the fulfillment of those promises surely seemed. God took a man a hundred years of age and renewed his body, making it young again. He took a woman ninety-plus years old and enabled her to give birth to a healthy boy. *"By faith Abraham obeyed…for he waited for the city which has foundations, whose builder and maker is God"* (Hebrews 11:8, 10). *"By faith Sarah herself also received strength to conceive seed, and she bore a child when she was past the age, because she judged Him faithful who had promised"* (verse 11).

When you continually affirm that Jesus is the surety of the new covenant and that every word from Genesis to Revelation can be utterly depended upon, then that Word on your lips is God speaking. When you say what God has told you to say, it is as though Jesus were saying it. When you remember that the Word never grows old, never weakens, never loses its power, but is always the living Word—the life-giving Word—and you boldly confess it, then it becomes a living thing on your lips.

Openly affirm that the Scriptures are what they profess to be—the very Word of God—and that God's Word is your contract as well as your contact with Him. Then the Word becomes a powerful, living reality in your daily life.

Your word can become one with God's Word. His Word can become one with your word. And His Word, abiding in you because of your unfailing affirmation of it, grants you authority in heaven. Jesus said, *"If you abide in Me, and My words abide in you, you will ask what you desire, and it shall be done for you"* (John 15:7). The words that abide in you and dominate you are the words on your lips. Make sure those words are the same as God's Word!

Prayer: Heavenly Father, I affirm my belief in Your Word and resolve to confirm it with my own words. I ask that You would steadily increase my faith and strengthen the power of Your Word in my daily life. In Jesus's name, amen.

Thought: Have you been using your words to dwell on doubt or to build faith by affirming belief?

Readings: Genesis 12:1–9; Hebrews 11:8–12

DAY 27

AFFIRM THAT GOD IS THE STRENGTH OF YOUR LIFE

The Lord is the strength of your *mind*, and so, today, affirm that you will think sound, healthy thoughts. Think upon those things that are true, honest, just, pure, lovely, and of a good report. (See Philippians 4:8.) A strong mind is a positive mind, the mind of Christ. Affirm the following: "[I] *have the mind of Christ*" (1 Corinthians 2:16).

The Lord is the strength of your *ears*, and so you shall hear well today. Seven times in chapters two and three of Revelation, we find this command: "*He who has an ear, let him hear what the Spirit says…*" (Revelation 2:7, 11, 17, 29; 3:6, 13, 22). With your mind that is strong, sound, and renewed, you hear what the Spirit says to you.

The Lord is the strength of your *eyes*, so you have good vision for today. Affirm that you see others through eyes of love, kindness, and goodwill.

The Lord is the strength of your *mouth*, so you will speak words that are edifying, ministering grace to those who hear you. Affirm Isaiah 50:4: "*The Lord God has given Me the tongue of the learned, that I should know how to speak a word in season to him who is weary. He awakens Me morning by morning, He awakens my ear to hear as the learned.*" Commit that you will refrain from speaking words that are negative, destructive, critical, corrupt, harsh, or unkind.

The Lord is the strength of your *heart*, so you have a good, sound heartbeat today. Let this be your prayer: "Lord, be the strength of my physical heart as long as I serve You on this earth—indeed, seventy years, and, by reason of strength, eighty or more." (See Psalm 90:10.) Command your heart to do its good work for this day.

The Lord is the strength of your *hands*, so that whatever your hands find to do, they will do it with all their might (see Ecclesiastes 9:10), "*heartily, as to the Lord and not to men*" (Colossians 3:23).

The Lord is the strength of every *organ, tissue, bone, fiber, nerve,* and *cell* in your body. The Lord is the strength of your life, from the top of your head to the soles of your feet. When your body becomes tired and starts to ache, the Lord shall renew your strength so that you may "*run and not be weary…walk and not faint*" (Isaiah 40:31).

The Lord is the strength of your *life*, your whole life—spirit, soul, and body. He infuses strength into the hidden places of the heart. He makes it so that the weak can say, "I am strong." (See Joel 3:10.) The joy of His very presence shall be your strength! (See Nehemiah 8:10.)

> *Prayer:* Heavenly Father, I praise You for being the strength of my life. Help me to forsake all other sources of strength and rely on You above all. In Jesus's name, amen.
>
> *Thought:* In what aspects of your life or body are you particularly aware of the Lord's strengthening presence today?
>
> *Readings:* Isaiah 40:10–31; Philippians 4:8–13

DAY 28

AVOID IDLE, MINDLESS CONFESSIONS

Jesus said, "*The words that I speak to you are spirit, and they are life*" (John 6:63). Are your own words bringing life or death to you? The answer lies in whether you are speaking discouragement and defeat or confidence and victory.

Suppose someone asks you, "How have you been getting along?" And your response is something along these lines: "Everything is going wrong! The bottom seems to have fallen out of everything. I've lost my grip. I can't seem to get past any of my problems."

Those kinds of statements amount to confessions that produce distinct reactions upon and within you.

Giving voice to a defeatist attitude only fills you with self-pity and reinforces your sense of defeat. It robs you of the power of initiative, the ability to pick up the scattered ends in your life and bring them together again in victory. You won't be able to do it. Why? Because your confession has unnerved you and wrecked your chances of recovering.

The same thing holds true when you encounter trouble in a relationship, such as with your spouse or a close friend. Every time you bemoan your troubles and verbally rehash the issues you are having, you go through the deepest agony that could have been avoided if you had only refused to declare your struggle and pronounce your problems.

Your words can be poison to your own system. They can prove deadly if you aren't careful.

When you say, "I don't believe I'll ever get over this illness," or "I doubt I'll ever reconcile with so-and-so," you are ingesting poison.

There is no antidote for this poison other than to break the power of that kind of negative confession and beginning instead to speak the right kind of words, declaring the right kind of confessions.

There are three classes of words. The first class consists in neutral, colorless, empty, soulless words. Such words characterize the general conversation of most people. They lack life and power; they have little to no impact on those who hear them. The second class of words includes constructive, edifying, healing words—words that inspire, thrill, and convey a strong sense of hope, love, and victory. The third class of words are destructive—words that tear down, conveying bitterness, envy, hatred, and death. Such words spring forth from a heart full of bitterness and are sent out to wound, blight, curse, and condemn.

Watch your words, ever striving to keep your conversation in the second class of words—those that build up yourself and others, promoting power and life, rather than cutting down and causing death. Use your words to change lives for the better, to bless, build, and encourage, leading yourself and others to master great achievements in Jesus's name.

Prayer: Father God, forgive me for failing to realize the impact of my words. By Your Holy Spirit, make me aware of any idle, deadly words I am using, and direct my thoughts and my tongue toward life-affirming words of encouragement and power. In Jesus's name, amen.

Thought: What class of words characterizes most of your speech? Do you need to work on changing that?

Readings: Proverbs 18:6–8, 13–21; James 3:1–12

DAY 29

SPEAK JUSTIFICATION, NOT CONDEMNATION

Jesus said, *"By your words you will be justified, and by your words you will be condemned"* (Matthew 12:37). You are justified when you say what the Bible says—what the Word of God records.

Along the same lines, you are condemned if you negate the Bible's truth with your own doubts. It is astounding the faith that God-fearing people put in the wrong things. They believe firmly in cancer, stomach ulcers, leukemia, and other serious diseases. Their faith in those diseases reaches a point where it dominates them. These people become slaves to the fear of such ailments. They get into the habit of confessing their weakness, and their confession only weakens them further.

They confess their lack of faith, and they are filled with doubts. They confess their fear, and they become ever more afraid. They confess they are getting sicker, and their ailments increase. They confess their lack of resources, and they built up within their minds a sense of lack that takes over their lives.

You need to align your confession with the truth of God's Word so that it justifies you rather than condemns you.

You are justified when you say, as it says in God's Word, *"As far as the east is from the west, so far has He removed our transgressions from us"* (Psalm 103:12). But you are condemned if you say something to the contrary, such as, "God is holding the sins of my youth against me."

You are justified when you say, as it says in God's Word, *"No evil shall befall* [me], *nor shall any plague come near* [my] *dwelling"* (Psalm 91:10). But you are condemned if you say, "I'm afraid! I don't feel safe."

You are justified when you say, as it says in God's Word, *"He who is in* [me] *is greater than he who is in the world"* (1 John 4:4). But you are condemned if you say, "The devil's power is just too much for me."

You are justified when you say, as it says in God's Word, *"Bless the* LORD, *O my soul…who heals all* [my] *diseases"* (Psalm 103:2–3). But you are condemned if you say, "My illness is getting worse. I don't think I'll ever recover."

It isn't pleasant to realize just how easily we can condemn ourselves with our own words. But, as the Bible says, *"Happy is he who does not condemn himself in what he approves"* (Romans 14:22). If we are not under condemnation, we can possess great confidence in the promises of God.

Prayer: Father God, please forgive me for the confessions I have made that have condemned me. Free me from bondage to fear and strengthen my resolve to make only the right confessions—those that align with Your Word and bring justification. In Jesus's name, amen.

Thought: Do your words justify or condemn you?

Readings: Psalm 91; 1 John 3:21–22

DAY 30

PROCLAIM SUCCESS, NOT FAILURE

If you think and talk failure, you will sink down to its level. Your words create an atmosphere that will either injure and break you or strengthen and empower you. Be sure to speak the latter, setting yourself up for success instead of failure.

We can take consolation in these words of God to Joshua as he stepped in to the role of leader of the Israelites: *"As I was with Moses, so I will be with you. I will not leave you or forsake you"* (Joshua 1:5). There is something so strong and victorious in God's counsel to Joshua that our hearts unconsciously return to it again and again.

The Lord continued His counsel to Joshua, giving him the following instructions:

> *This Book of the Law shall not depart from your mouth, but you shall meditate in it day and night, that you may observe to do according to all that is written in it. For then you will make your way prosperous, and then you will have good success.*
> (Joshua 1:8)

Here is the secret of all success, whether spiritual, financial, physical, or another type: devote yourself to know the Book and know Him who inspired the Book. Find out His will and then live in it and do it.

A life walked with God becomes a drama, a romance. After a while, a sense of His omnipotence will overtake your spirit, and Philippians 4:13 will become a battle-ax with which you can smash every barrier between you and success: *"I can do all things through Christ who strengthens me."*

Your success is God's success. If you were to fail, it would be His failure. Fear not, for He is backing you, and His eye is upon you.

Accordingly, speak success, not failure! Confess that you possess impossibilities becoming realities because you are linked up with God by divine birth, and *"with God nothing will be impossible"* (Luke 1:37).

Confess that you possess supernatural help for every situation because your help *"comes from the LORD, who made heaven and earth"* (Psalm 121:2).

Confess your assurance that your labors for the Lord are fruitful, for you cling to 1 Corinthians 15:58: *"Be steadfast, immovable, always abounding in the work of the Lord, knowing that your labor is not in vain in the Lord."*

Faith doesn't ask for possible things. Faith demands the impossible. *"He who did not spare His own Son, but delivered Him up for us all, how shall He not with Him also freely give us all things?"* (Romans 8:32). When you cling to God's Word, you launch into the realm of the impossible, just as Abraham did when he believed God for a son. You're not asking for something that you can secure for yourself but for something beyond reason. And then, you refuse to entertain doubts or dwell on fears.

The greatest battles we win are those that seemed impossible—where there was the greatest opposition, where reason was discredited by faith. Hold fast to your confession of success over failure, and the Word is made good.

Prayer: Lord God, help me to hold fast to my confession of success and not failure. I refuse to succumb to defeatist thoughts but will only proclaim the victory I have in You. In Jesus's name, amen.

Thought: What impossible situation are you facing today that you need to face with confidence in your victory in Jesus?

Readings: Deuteronomy 20:4; Colossians 2:13–15

DAY 31

RIGHT AND WRONG CONFESSIONS ON THE JOB

You can't expect to succeed if you make the wrong confessions about your job and workplace. The wrong confession might be something like this: "Well, I made it to work today, but that's about all I can say. With the way I feel, I certainly don't expect to get much done." You need to conquer your negativity and make a positive confession that's built on the Word of God.

A positive confession might go something like this:

"I refuse to give place to a gloomy confession that would snare my soul beyond all hope. Proverbs 6:2 says, *'You are snared by the words of your mouth.'* Therefore, I say that because I serve God continually, I am assured of deliverance from such a pessimistic attitude that would crush my spirit and defeat my soul. After all, it says in Daniel 6:16, *'Your God, whom you serve continually, He will deliver you.'* God is my Deliverer in every situation, for I serve Him constantly. *'Thanks be to God who always leads us in triumph in Christ'* (2 Corinthians 2:14). On my job, in my home, in my service for the Lord—in whatever I do— Romans 8:37 tells me that I am more than a conqueror through Christ who loves me. I reject the attitude that leaves me barely able to keep my head above water. God is showing me great and mighty things in life, for He has promised, *'Call to Me, and I will answer you, and show you great and mighty things, which you do not know'* (Jeremiah 33:3). I call to Him; He is answering me and is showing me great and mighty things."

Here is another negative confession someone might make about work: "I failed to get that promotion I had hoped for, but it's just as I expected. I never seem to succeed at anything." A right confession to counter it might go as follows:

"I don't believe that any adverse forces are overthrowing God's work on my behalf or His great plans for me. The Lord is working on the answers even before I pray to Him, for He has said, *'Before they call, I will answer; and while they are still speaking, I will hear'* (Isaiah 65:24). I do not expect failure; I expect success. Jesus didn't come to give me a lackluster life. He said, *'I have come that they may have life, and that they may have it more abundantly'* (John 10:10). Because I have received Jesus Christ as my Savior and Lord, I have that abundant life in me right now. I know that God is prospering my life for His Word says, *'Beloved, I pray that you may prosper in all things and be in health, just as your soul prospers'* (3 John 1:2). I have a right to prosperity, and I am prospering in my soul."

Speak financial success rather than poverty and despair. *"Then you will make your way prosperous, and then you will have good success"* (Joshua 1:8).

Prayer: Father God, thank You for giving me a right to prosper on my job. Help me to do my best to bring You glory and to stand in confidence that You will meet and even exceed all my needs. In Jesus's name, amen.

Thought: Does your attitude toward your work and income need an adjustment?

Readings: Daniel 6:16–23; Colossians 3:17

DAY 32

PROCLAIM HEALTH, NOT SICKNESS

Our words have a profound impact on our health. People enslaved by illness have a tendency to say, "I'm getting a cold," or "I fear I'm coming down with the flu," or "I'm not feeling so well today." On the other hand, people who walk in divine health proclaim, for example, "I am rarely ill because germs can't reach me. I refuse to give in to illness."

Speak that you have the life of God in your mortal body, no longer the old spirit of inferiority, failure, and frustration. Remember that it's in Christ that *"we live and move and have our being"* (Acts 17:28).

Speak healing and health, not sickness and disease. Isaiah 33:24 talks about a future time when *"the inhabitant will not say, 'I am sick.'"* That verse gives us a good practice for faith-filled living. Don't say, "I am sick," but speak the Word that affirms your healing: "With His stripes, I am healed." (See Isaiah 53:5.)

Confess your dominion over disease in Jesus's name. Never be frightened by any condition, no matter how intimidating or impossible the case may seem. It may be cancer, an allergy, or an accident in which death seems to be the master of the situation. No matter what, you must never give in to fear. Never forget that you and God are masters of the situation. Never for even one moment lose the confession of your supremacy over the works of the devil. This disease or calamity is not of God. It has but one source: Satan.

In Jesus's name, you are master. You have taken Jesus's place; you act in His stead. Fearlessly take your position and confess your ability in Christ to meet any emergency. Always remember that Jesus met defeat and conquered it. Every defeat you face, you face as its master.

Prayer: Lord, I boldly confess my belief that Jesus carried my sicknesses to the cross and defeated them on Calvary. Help me to hold fast to this confession and to trust You for my healing. In Jesus's name, amen.

Thought: Are you confident of healing, or do you tend to be a hypochondriac?

Readings: Psalm 107:20–22; Acts 5:12–16

DAY 33

THE ALPHABET OF HEALING

Don ministered healing to many people in many different circumstances. There were occasions when he had ample time for deep intercessions to drive out the spirit of infirmity, and other occasions when time was short and he had to draw on something he developed for situations when time was of the essence. He called it his *alphabet of healing*.

You can affirm any one of these twenty-six Scriptures to expel a spirit of disease and find a healing portion with little effort.

A: *"**Attend** to my words; incline thine ear unto my sayings. Let them not depart from thine eyes…for they are life unto those that find them, and health to all their flesh"* (Proverbs 4:20–22 kjv).

B: *"**Beloved**, I pray that you may prosper in all things and be in health, just as your soul prospers"* (3 John 1:2).

C: *"**Create** in me a clean heart, O God, and renew a steadfast spirit within me"* (Psalm 51:10).

D: *"**Deal** bountifully with Your servant, that I may live and keep Your word"* (Psalm 119:17).

E: *"The **effective**, fervent prayer of a righteous man avails much"* (James 5:16).

F: *"**Forget** not all His benefits: who forgives all your iniquities, who heals all your diseases"* (Psalm 103:2–3).

G: "**God** *anointed Jesus of Nazareth with the Holy Spirit and with power, who went about doing good and healing all who were oppressed by the devil, for* **God** *was with Him*" (Acts 10:38).

H: "**He Himself** [Jesus] *took our infirmities and bore our sicknesses*" (Matthew 8:17).

I: "**I** *am the* Lord *who heals you*" (Exodus 15:26).

J: "**Jesus** *Christ is the same yesterday, today, and forever*" (Hebrews 13:8).

K: "**Know** *ye not that your body is the temple of the Holy Ghost which is in you, which ye have of God, and ye are not your own? For ye are bought with a price: therefore glorify God in your body, and in your spirit, which are God's*" (1 Corinthians 6:19–20 kjv).

L: "**Lay** *hands on the sick, and they will recover*" (Mark 16:18).

M: "*A* **merry** *heart does good, like medicine*" (Proverbs 17:22).

N: "*His* [Jesus's] **name,** *through faith in His* **name,** *has made this man strong, whom you see and know. Yes, the faith which comes through Him has given him this perfect soundness in the presence of you all*" (Acts 3:16).

O: "**Ought** *not this woman, being a daughter of Abraham, whom Satan has bound—think of it—for eighteen years, be loosed from this bond?*" (Luke 13:16).

P: "*The* **power** *of the Lord was present to heal them*" (Luke 5:17).

Q: "*If the Spirit of him that raised up Jesus from the dead dwell in you, he that raised up Christ from the dead shall also* **quicken** *your mortal bodies by his Spirit that dwelleth in you*" (Romans 8:11 kjv).

R: "**Resist** *the devil and he will flee from you*" (James 4:7).

S: "[God] *sent* His word and healed them, and delivered them from all their destructions" (Psalm 107:20).

T: "*Talk* of all His wondrous works!" (Psalm 105:2).

U: "*Unto* you that fear my name shall the Sun of righteousness arise with healing in his wings" (Malachi 4:2 KJV).

V: "The whole multitude sought to touch [Jesus]: for there went *virtue* out of him, and healed them all" (Luke 6:19 KJV).

W: "*With* his stripes we are healed" (Isaiah 53:5 KJV).

X: "My soul, wait silently for God alone, for my *expectation* is from Him" (Psalm 62:5).

Y: "[God] *satisfies* your mouth with good things, so that your *youth* is renewed like the eagle's" (Psalm 103:5).

Z: "The LORD will be *zealous* for His land, and pity His people" (Joel 2:18).

If you are in need of healing, affirm all twenty-six of the Bible verses listed here. They contain God's healing provisions for your spirit, soul, and body. Believe and receive your healing!

Prayer: Heavenly Father, thank You for making such wonderful provision for my healing. Help me to stand on the countless promises in Your Word as I wait for the manifestation of the healing You have already performed for me. In Jesus's name, amen.

Thought: Which of these twenty-six Scriptures resonated with you the most?

Readings: Exodus 15:25–26; Acts 28:8–10

DAY 34

PROCLAIM VICTORY, NOT DEFEAT

Your words can work wonders, but they can also work blunders. Do you realize that multitudes of people fail and fall into defeat because they have been speaking failure and loss rather than success and victory? They fear failure, and so they allow their fear to overrule their faith.

What you say determines your location. You will not—you cannot—rise above your words. If you speak defeat, failure, anxiety, sickness, and unbelief, you will live on that level. No one, no matter how clever, will ever live higher than the standard of their conversation. This is an unalterable spiritual principle.

If you think back on the troubles you have encountered and the places where you have experienced defeat, you will probably agree that the common thread through all those struggles is the words you have spoken. Remember, *"Whoever guards his mouth and tongue keeps his soul from troubles"* (Proverbs 21:23).

You cannot be conquered as long as you control your thoughts and your words, thinking and proclaiming only victory and never defeat. In your spirit and with your mouth, always affirm, "I am more than a conqueror." (See Romans 8:37.)

God and you together are victors. Greater is He who is in you than any opposition or disease. (See 1 John 4:4.) There is no trouble and no disease that is greater than our God. There is no lack that He cannot meet, no obstacle He cannot overcome. This indomitable will that God has brought about in you cannot be overwhelmed or conquered.

Always remember what you are: a new creation, a branch of the true Vine, an heir of God. You are united with Him. You and He are one; of course, He is the greater part of that one.

You are one of God's instruments. There is no such thing as conquering God when His instruments refuse to admit that the enemy can overwhelm them.

Never fear failure. Never talk defeat. Never for a moment entertain or proclaim the erroneous idea that God's ability is insufficient to put you over your circumstances. Remember at all times that He who is in you is greater than any force that could come against you. He is the God who created a universe with words—words that are mightier than any tank, bomb, or army. Tap into that might by speaking only victory and never defeat!

Prayer: Father God, I boldly confess that because You live within me, I am more than a conqueror over any obstacle and enemy that would oppose me. May I ever stand confident of my victory in You and declare that victory without wavering. In Jesus's name, amen.

Thought: What struggles have had you cowering in fear? How will you now face them, confident of your victory through Jesus?

Readings: Psalm 17; Revelation 12:10–11

DAY 35

PROCLAIM STRENGTH, NOT WEAKNESS

Let the weak say, 'I am strong'" (Joel 3:10). You are strong! This is the paradox of faith: to say that you are strong when you are weak. This is faith's confession: "I am strong."

No matter what you think of yourself, you are strong. Regardless of others' opinions about you and your life, you are strong. Even when you feel the weakest, you are strong.

In spite of past experiences of succumbing to weakness, you can rise up with a new testimony of faith: "I am strong." It is not just when you feel strong that you should say you are strong; again, it is even when you feel weak that you must declare, "I am strong."

God commands you to say that you are strong. By doing so, you say the same thing that God says about you. You are using the language of faith, the language of victory.

Who are you? You are strong. Whatever else you may be, you are strong. Wherever you are, you are strong. Whatever you are doing, you are strong.

What you confess, you possess. What you say is what you get. Boldly confess, "I am strong," and you will possess strength.

Why can you be so sure of being strong? Not only in Joel 3:10, but also in countless other Scripture verses, God declares Himself to be your strength. So, you should gladly obey His command and say, "I am strong." Never say, "I am weak," for doing so would be to disobey God and would grieve the Holy Spirit.

"*Let the weak say, 'I am strong'*" (Joel 3:10). What are you fearing today? Do you fear an untimely death? Are you afraid of suffering a heart attack? Is your fear of cancer? Do you fear calamity of some sort? Do you fear the loss of the affection of your loved ones? Do you have a dread of flying in airplanes? Is the fear of man prevalent in your life?

If there is any fear in your heart, you must be freed from it. Fear is an actual spirit that moves from without to take up occupancy in a life. Satan takes advantage of our giving place to fear and sees that the thing we fear is reproduced in our lives.

We read in Job 3:25 these words of the title character of that Bible book: "*The thing I greatly feared has come upon me, and what I dreaded has happened to me.*" Job made this confession when he was on the ash heap of great suffering, with boils afflicting him from the top of his head to the soles of his feet—after he had lost his entire family and all his earthly possessions. Job evidently had entertained this fear for a long time, given his admission that "*the thing I greatly feared has come upon me, and what I dreaded has happened to me.*"

What are you fearing today? What has you quaking in your shoes, feeling weak and vulnerable? You must expel every spirit of fear from your life, or else that negative, tormenting fear may reproduce into your life the very thing that you fear.

Luke 1:74–75 explains that one purpose of Christ's coming to the world was "*to grant us that we, being delivered from the hand of our enemies, might serve Him without fear...all the days of our life.*" This means that you should be free every day from feelings of fear, weakness, and vulnerability. Boldly proclaim this right now: "You satanic spirit of fear that is oppressing and vexing me, I command you in Jesus's name to depart from my life, because it is written:

'God has not given us a spirit of fear, but of power and of love and of a sound mind' (2 Timothy 1:7)."

> **Prayer:** Heavenly Father, You are my strength, and so I declare today, "I am strong; I need not fear." Help me to consider myself strong even when I'm not feeling that way. In Jesus's name, amen.
>
> **Thought:** In what areas have you often considered yourself to be weak and fearful? How can you turn those around today by remembering that you are strong in the Lord?
>
> **Readings:** Psalm 27; 2 Timothy 1:3–7

DAY 36

WHAT YOU ARE NOT

You are not sick, for the Lord heals you of all your diseases. (See Psalm 103:3.)

You are not bound, for the Son has made you free indeed. (See John 8:36.)

You are not defeated, for you're more than a conqueror through Jesus Christ who loves you. (See Romans 8:37.)

You are not weak, for *"the LORD will give strength to His people"* (Psalm 29:11).

You do not lack power, for *"you shall receive power when the Holy Spirit has come upon you"* (Acts 1:8).

You are not without peace, for *"having been justified by faith, we have peace with God through our Lord Jesus Christ"* (Romans 5:1).

You lack no good thing, for *"no good thing will [God] withhold from those who walk uprightly"* (Psalm 84:11).

You are not overtaken by any evil work, for *"the Lord will deliver [you] from every evil work and preserve [you] for His heavenly kingdom"* (2 Timothy 4:18).

You are not afraid of any plague, for *"no evil shall befall you, nor shall any plague come near your dwelling"* (Psalm 91:10).

You are not running from the devil, for you are resisting the devil, and he is fleeing from you. (See James 4:7.)

You are not shackled by sin, demons, or fear, for *"your God, whom you serve continually, He will deliver you"* (Daniel 6:16).

You are not in a losing battle, for *"the Lord will fight for you, and you shall hold your peace"* (Exodus 14:14).

You are not without joy, for the joy of the Lord is within you, and your joy shall be full. (See John 15:11.)

You are not failing to see God, for *"blessed are the pure in heart, for they shall see God"* (Matthew 5:8).

You are not oppressed by cares, difficulties, and troubles, for you are *"casting all your care upon* [God], *for He cares for you"* (1 Peter 5:7).

Prayer: God, help me to remember *what I am not* because of the wonderful truths of Your Word. I am Your child, redeemed, beloved, and protected for all eternity. In Jesus's name, amen.

Thought: Which of these "you are nots" resonated the most with you? Why do you suppose that is?

Readings: Daniel 6:10–23; Matthew 5:1–12

DAY 37

EVEN WHEN YOU
DON'T FEEL IT, SAY IT

What you say is what you get. In the words of Jesus, "*who-ever…believes that those things he says will be done, he will have whatever he says*" (Mark 11:23). What you confess is what you possess. As we have established, your confession of God's Word precedes your possession of the promises therein. Therefore, it is essential to speak rightly, even if you don't yet feel in your mind or heart the reality or the manifestation of those promises.

When you need healing, speak aloud as often as you can, "By His stripes I am healed." (See Isaiah 53:5; 1 Peter 2:24.) Say it when you feel like saying it. Say it *especially* when you don't feel like saying it. Say it with all the confidence you can muster, at every time of the day.

When you feel weak, proclaim Psalm 27:1, "*The Lord is the strength of my life,*" and Philippians 4:13, "*I can do all things through Christ who strengthens me.*" Say these things when you feel well and strong, but especially say them when you are feeling weak and defeated. Say it whether you are on the mountaintop of spiritual blessing or in the valley of melancholy and despair.

When you are fearful, speak 2 Timothy 1:7 with authority: "*God has not given* [me] *a spirit of fear, but of power and of love and of a sound mind.*" Speak up and see your fears vanish. Feeling or no feeling, you know that "*the word of God…lives and abides forever*" (1 Peter 1:23), and your standing upon that foundation is sure.

When you are tempted to doubt God's Word, you must doubt your doubt, for doubt is of the devil. You are a believer, and if you believe, you receive; if you doubt, you do without. Speak Romans 12:3 with bold assurance: *"God has dealt to each one a measure of faith."* Affirm that faith is something you have, and faith describes what you actually believe in the depths of your heart.

When you lack money or other resources, boldly declare Philippians 4:19: *"My God shall supply all [my] need according to His riches in glory by Christ Jesus."* Say it when you have enough money in the bank, and say it when your account is empty. Say it when your senses register that you are prospering, and say it when it appears that you are stricken by poverty.

Speak God's Word often.

This Book of the Law shall not depart from your mouth, but you shall meditate in it day and night, that you may observe to do according to all that is written in it. For then you will make your way prosperous, and then you will have good success.
(Joshua 1:8)

Morning, noon, and night, and often in between, speak God's Word. This is the greatest form of self-discipline in which you can engage—to speak God's Word at all times, under all circumstances. Think on God's Word in silence, and speak it aloud as often as possible. Proclaim it when the pressure from the enemy is upon you, and say it when you are basking in the presence of the Spirit. Say it when you feel like saying it, and say it *especially* when you don't feel like saying it!

Blessed is the man…[whose] delight is in the law of the LORD…whatever he does shall prosper. (Psalm 1:1–3)

Prayer: Father God, I confess that I don't always have confidence in Your Word or always feel like proclaiming Your promises, but help me to make a habit of doing so regardless of how I feel. Give me the self-discipline to study, meditate on, and proclaim Your Word day and night, so that I might have success in all that You lead me to do. In Jesus's name, amen.

Thought: In what kinds of circumstances do you least feel like saying what you believe? Make a conscious effort to overcome your feelings and proclaim the Word regardless!

Readings: Psalm 1; Philippians 4:4–9

DAY 38

YOUR "NEVER AGAIN" LIST

Never again should you confess that you cannot do something; proclaim instead, "*I can do all things through Christ who strengthens me*" (Philippians 4:13).

Never again should you confess lack; proclaim instead, "*My God shall supply all* [my] *need according to His riches in glory by Christ Jesus*" (Philippians 4:19).

Never again should you confess fear; proclaim instead, "*God has not given* [me] *a spirit of fear, but of power and of love and of a sound mind*" (2 Timothy 1:7).

Never again should you confess doubt and lack of faith; proclaim instead, "*God has dealt to each one a measure of faith*" (Romans 12:3).

Never again should you confess weakness; proclaim instead, "*The* LORD *is the strength of my life*" (Psalm 27:1), and "*The people who know their God shall be strong, and carry out great exploits*" (Daniel 11:32).

Never again should you confess the supremacy of Satan over your life; proclaim instead, "*He who is in* [me] *is greater than he who is in the world*" (1 John 4:4).

Never again should you confess lack of wisdom; proclaim instead, "*Christ Jesus…became for us wisdom from God*" (1 Corinthians 1:30).

Never again should you confess sickness; proclaim instead, "*By His stripes* [I am] *healed*" (Isaiah 53:5), and "[Jesus] *Himself took our infirmities and bore our sicknesses*" (Matthew 8:17).

Never again should you confess worries and frustrations; proclaim instead, "I am casting all my care upon God, for He cares for me." (See 1 Peter 5:7.)

Never again should you confess bondage; proclaim instead, "*Where the Spirit of the Lord is, there is liberty*" (2 Corinthians 3:17), and "My body '*is the temple of the Holy Spirit*'" (1 Corinthians 6:19).

Never again should you confess condemnation; proclaim instead, "*There is therefore now no condemnation to those who are in Christ Jesus*" (Romans 8:1).

Never again should you confess loneliness; proclaim instead, "I am never alone, for Jesus has said, '*I am with you always, even to the end of the age*'" (Matthew 28:20), and "*I will never leave you nor forsake you*" (Hebrews 13:5).

Never again should you confess curses and bad luck; proclaim instead, "*Christ has redeemed us from the curse of the law, having become a curse for us...that we might receive the promise of the Spirit through faith*" (Galatians 3:13–14).

Never again should you confess discontent; proclaim instead, "*I have learned in whatever state I am, to be content*" (Philippians 4:11).

Never again should you confess confusion; proclaim instead, "*God is not the author of confusion but of peace*" (1 Corinthians 14:33).

Never again should you confess the dominion of sin over your life; proclaim instead, "*The law of the Spirit of life in Christ Jesus has made me free from the law of sin and death*" (Romans 8:2).

Never again should you confess fear of the future; proclaim instead, *"Eye has not seen, nor ear heard, nor have entered into the heart of man the things which God has prepared for those who love Him"* (1 Corinthians 2:9).

> **Prayer:** Father God, forgive me for making negative, doubt-filled confessions that contradict Your Word. Help me to speak only what Your Word says and not voice expressions of doubt or fear. In Jesus's name, amen.
>
> **Thought:** What are some things you've been saying routinely that you recognized on this "never again" list?
>
> **Readings:** Psalm 103; Romans 8:28–39

PART IV

LIVING WITH BOLD FAITH

"Christ lives in me, and I live by faith in Him who loved me and gave Himself for me."
See Galatians 2:20.

LIVING WITH THE SPIRIT OF FAITH

Living in God's power means living with the spirit of faith. What is the spirit of faith? The apostle Paul described it by quoting Psalm 116:10, saying, *"Since we have the same spirit of faith, according to what is written, 'I believed and therefore I spoke,' we also believe and therefore speak"* (2 Corinthians 4:13).

The spirit of faith is something we have, something we possess. We are men and women of faith. The Bible makes it clear that God has given to each person *"a measure of faith"* (Romans 12:3). As Christians, we are not a bunch of doubters; we have been born again into *"the household of faith"* (Galatians 6:10).

Living the life of true faith means believing the Word in your heart and speaking or confessing the Word with your mouth. It means living a life about which it can be said, *"'The word is near you, in your mouth and in your heart' (that is, the word of faith which we preach)"* (Romans 10:8).

The person with the spirit of faith can boldly make this confession: "I believe the Word of God; therefore, as I speak the Word of God, I am a member of the household of faith. God has given me *'a measure of faith.'* I never speak of doubt, for I am a believer. The Word is near me, in my heart and in my mouth. Through the word of faith, I am a victor, because faith is the victory!"

The secret of victory is grasping your problem firmly with both hands. The secret of winning is facing the difficulty with a consciousness that it cannot whip you because it cannot whip God. The way to face an impossible situation is to realize that you are linked with God, and he who is linked with God can no more fail than God can fail.

The faith that Jesus had in Himself, in His ministry, and in His Father enabled Him to face the cross with the spirit of a conqueror. When you are linked with God, the resources of God belong to you. God underwrites every enterprise into which He sends you.

You may not feel the thrill and emotion that you would think is natural when one is linked with omnipotence. But you do not need to feel it. All you need to know is that greater is He who is in you, who is energizing you and empowering you, than all the opposition that could possibly come against you. (See 1 John 4:4.) Then you can face life's problems and difficulties with a holy calmness and a boldness backed by almighty God.

> *Prayer:* Father, thank You for my rebirth into the household of faith. Help me to live boldly by the spirit of faith, confident that because You are in me, I can conquer anything. In Jesus's name, amen.
>
> *Thought:* Have you been placing too much emphasis on the measure of faith you think you have? Or are you confident in God's presence no matter how you may feel?
>
> *Readings:* Psalm 8; 1 John 4:12–16

DAY 40

BOLDNESS BASED ON THE WORD

Boldness is not the same as arrogance, bravado, or pretense. It is courage; it is confidence; it is faith in God. It is a settled conviction that He who strengthens your arm and guides your work is greater than any force that either humans or demons could bring against you. Boldness is the silent assurance that with God on your side, you must prevail.

Boldness is born of a conscious union with God—a confidence that you are doing His will, achieving His desire, and carrying forward His program. All the faculties of your being have been lined up with God, and you act in full dependence on His wisdom, grace, and power.

Faith is enabling you to face life's problems with a smile. Faith in Him, the unseen One, has lifted you out of your weakness and into the sphere of His strength. He is your life, for you are hidden with Christ in God. (See Colossians 3:3.)

In light of this fact, we can *"come boldly to the throne of grace, that we may obtain mercy and find grace to help in time of need"* (Hebrews 4:16). This is because we come in the name of Jesus, with lips full of His Word. We come boldly to the throne in the name of Jesus and in the authority of His own promise that *"whatever you ask the Father in My name He will give you"* (John 16:23).

This verse means that Jesus utters the prayers that our own lips are saying. And Jesus has said, *"If two of you agree on earth concerning anything that they ask, it will be done for them by My Father in heaven"* (Matthew 18:19). When we quote His Word, it is His Word going up before the Father. It is His prayer, not our prayer.

Jesus also said, *"If you abide in Me, and My words abide in you, you will ask what you desire, and it shall be done for you"* (John 15:7). When we pray with Jesus's words, the Father hears the words of Jesus coming from lips that are yielded to the lordship of His Son. We remind Him that the Word abides in us and that we abide in Him. It is the Master Himself doing the talking.

Jesus prays through us! So, we can quote John 14:13 before the Father: *"Whatever you ask in My name, that I will do, that the Father may be glorified in the Son."* We say to the Father, "I desire that You will be glorified through Jesus, so I am asking in Jesus's name that such and such a thing be done."

The word *"ask"* can also mean "demand." We demand, for example, that a sickness leave someone's body. We know that when this takes place, the Father is glorified. We take Jesus's side of the issue and do the thing that will glorify the Father.

When we assume this attitude, prayer becomes a God-sized affair. We enter into the fullness of Christ in our prayer lives. Wherever we are, whatever we are doing, we can send angelic forces to minister to those in need when we use Jesus's words on our lips, because it is as if the Master Himself were present and speaking these words. This is the basis of bold faith.

Prayer: Heavenly Father, please give me the confidence to come boldly before Your throne of grace and use the words of Jesus to make my requests. I know that You hear me, and I desire to glorify You with my every prayer. In Jesus's name, amen.

Thought: Have you been underestimating the power of Jesus's words in your mouth?

Readings: Deuteronomy 18:17–19; Colossians 3:16–17

DAY 41

AGREEING WITH GOD

You cannot truly walk with God and live a life of powerful faith unless you agree with Him. *"Can two walk together, unless they are agreed?"* (Amos 3:3). To agree with God is to say the same thing God says in His Word about salvation, healing, prayer, and living an overcoming life.

You agree with God first of all by saying that you are who God has said you are: His child, a new creation in Christ. *"If anyone is in Christ, he is a new creation; old things have passed away; behold, all things have become new"* (2 Corinthians 5:17). You also say that you are *"more than a conqueror"* through Christ. (See Romans 8:37.) You disagree with the devil, who would try to convince you that you are a failure, a weakling, or a sinner beyond saving.

How can you walk with God in a way that lets you experience His blessings and exercise His power? By agreeing with God that you have what He says you have: His name, His nature, His power, His authority, and His love. You agree that you have what God has said in His Word is yours.

Just as Enoch *"walked with God"* (Genesis 5:22), so you can walk with God by agreeing that you have been given the ability to do what He says you can do: witness with power, cast out demons, and minister His healing power to people. Your testimony should be that *"I can do all things through Christ who strengthens me"* (Philippians 4:13). You must agree that you can do what God has said in His Word that you can do.

If you speak only what your senses dictate, you will not agree with God. You must agree with God by speaking His Word. It is the confession of faith that is your victory.

To walk with God, you must *disagree* with the devil. Jesus did this very thing when the devil tried to tempt Him in the wilderness and He boldly declared, *"It is written…"* (Matthew 4:4, 7, 10). He resisted the devil by quoting the Word, and we can do the same.

Walk daily with God by agreeing with Him and His Word. Because He has said it, we may boldly say it!

Prayer: Father God, I want to agree with You at all times, always echoing Your Word and confirming its truths. Silence the voice of disagreement within me, so that I may walk continually in accord with You. In Jesus's name, amen.

Thought: On what points have you recently disagreed with God? How can you change your thinking and your speech to agree with Him today?

Readings: Nehemiah 8:1–6; Matthew 4:1–11

DAY 42

BOLD BIBLE LIVING, PART I

Those who know the Father should exemplify what we call "bold Bible living." The first aspect of bold Bible living is *living boldly*. *"He who has the Son has life"* (1 John 5:12). When we receive Christ as our Lord and Savior, God gives us *life* abundant (see John 10:10) and *life* everlasting (see John 3:16).

Second, bold Bible living means living according to the Bible. Jesus described how to live this way when He said, *"Man shall not live by bread alone, but by every word that proceeds from the mouth of God"* (Matthew 4:4). Living by God's Word is bold Bible living.

Third, bold Bible living must exhibit the boldness that God has commanded His children to exercise. *"The righteous are bold as a lion"* (Proverbs 28:1). Who are the righteous? All born-again Christians. And how are they righteous? By virtue of their faith in Jesus Christ. We have no righteousness of our own that can please God, but God *"made Him who knew no sin to be sin for us, that we might become the righteousness of God in Him"* (2 Corinthians 5:21). Yes, you are the righteousness of the Lord—therefore, you can be as bold as a lion!

What does it mean to be *"bold as a lion"*? It primarily means exhibiting these four attributes: confidence, courage, fearlessness, and daring.

Your *confidence* should be confidence in Christ rather than in yourself—a confidence that enables you to shout, *"I can do all things through Christ who strengthens me"* (Philippians 4:13).

Your *courage* should be the courage that characterized all the righteous ones in the Bible. Consider the deeds of such brave individuals as Daniel, David, Elijah, Abraham, Joshua, Rahab, Moses, and Esther, to name just a few.

Fearlessness is the ability of God that empowers us to live free from fear and anxiety all our days. *"For God has not given us a spirit of fear, but of power and of love and of a sound mind"* (2 Timothy 1:7).

Daring refers to our acting on the Word of God, to do with conviction that which God says we can do.

These four qualities are distinct, yet they harmonize together in the person who exemplifies bold Bible living. It is difficult to have one without possessing all four of them.

Prayer: Lord God, thank You for the incredible gift of abundant life that was bought for me by Your Son Jesus. Help me to embrace that life with boldness and to live by Your Word. In Jesus's name, amen.

Thought: In what areas can you live more like a bold lion?

Readings: Proverbs 28:1; 1 John 5:1–5

DAY 43

BOLD BIBLE LIVING, PART II

The Word of God abounds with challenging truths to assure us that God gives us the qualities of confidence, courage, fearlessness, and daring—and then expects us to put them to use. For example, consider the following verses:

> *Fear not, for I am with you; be not dismayed, for I am your God.* (Isaiah 41:10)
>
> *In quietness and confidence shall be your strength.* (Isaiah 30:15)
>
> *Be strong and of good courage; do not be afraid, nor be dismayed, for the LORD your God is with you wherever you go.* (Joshua 1:9)

This is bold Bible living: being courageous in the midst of all types of adversity and realizing that the triumphant are those who practice this truth. It is being able to say with David, *"Though an army may encamp against me, my heart shall not fear; though war may rise against me, in this I will be confident"* (Psalm 27:3).

If ever a man displayed confidence, courage, fearlessness, and daring, it was David when he came to the rescue of the Israelite army against Goliath. The entire army was paralyzed by fear of that Philistine giant. No man would do battle with him. Every last soldier cowered in his presence and in the face of his humiliating taunts. So overwhelming were the odds against the Israelite army that no man would even attempt to save face in that time of crisis.

Yet we see David step out onto that field of battle and challenge Goliath, even as the giant laughed at him. David was no coward. God had granted him victories in the past against such formidable foes as lions and bears. (See 1 Samuel 17:34–37.) This young man possessed confidence, courage, fearlessness, and daring.

By the help of his God, David conquered the giant. What were the secrets to his success? First, he believed in his heart that he could conquer Goliath, and he boldly declared the same. (See 1 Samuel 17:45–47.) You, too, must proclaim your faith, confess the Scriptures, and boldly affirm that what God has spoken is yours.

Second, David drew his strength from the name of the Lord. He declared to Goliath, "*I come to you in the name of the Lord of hosts, the God of the armies of Israel*" (verse 45). Your strength must be in the name of the Lord. "*The name of the Lord is a strong tower; the righteous run to it and are safe*" (Proverbs 18:10).

Third, David feared the Lord—that is, he revered His power and recognized His omnipotent abilities—more than he feared Goliath. Because his fear of God eclipsed his fear of man, he was able to say of the giant, when everyone else was quaking in his boots, "*Who is this uncircumcised Philistine, that he should defy the armies of the living God?...Let no man's heart fail because of him; your servant will go and fight with this Philistine*" (1 Samuel 17:26, 32).

Fourth, David possessed a sense of daring that stemmed from his assurance that God would come through for him, just as He had promised. Accordingly, David was able tell Goliath:

This day the Lord will deliver you into my hand, and I will strike you and take your head from you. And this day I will give the carcasses of the camp of the Philistines to the birds of the air and the wild beasts of the earth, that all the earth may

know that there is a God in Israel. Then all this assembly shall know that the Lord *does not save with sword and spear; for the battle is the* Lord's, *and He will give you into our hands.*
(1 Samuel 17:46–47)

Prayer: Lord God, give me the confidence, courage, fearlessness, and daring of David. Strengthen me by Your name against all enemies and adversities, that I might display bold Bible living all my days. In Jesus's name, amen.

Thought: What giants are you facing today that you can conquer with the confidence, courage, fearlessness, and daring that God gives?

Readings: Psalm 71; Ephesians 6:10–18

DAY 44

ANY MEASURE OF FAITH
IS ENOUGH

Never call yourself a "doubting Thomas," or you risk closing the door on the provisions of God for you in Christ. Never chide yourself for "not having enough faith." It was by faith that you became God's child in the first place: *"For you are all sons of God through faith in Christ Jesus"* (Galatians 3:26).

Where did the faith come from that made you a child of God? *"By grace you have been saved through faith, and that **not of yourselves; it is the gift of God**"* (Ephesians 2:8). There is no disputing the fact that God has given you your measure of faith: *"God has dealt to each one a measure of faith"* (Romans 12:3). It does not matter how much faith you may have; quantity of faith is not what is important to Jesus, who declared that even faith as small as a mustard seed can move a mountain. (See Matthew 17:20.)

Not only do you have the measure of faith God has given you, but you also have the spirit of faith: *"Since we have the same spirit of faith, according to what is written, 'I believed and therefore I spoke,' we also believe and therefore speak"* (2 Corinthians 4:13). This spirit of faith that you have is expressed by your believing in your heart and speaking with your mouth.

Faith is not a magic button that you can press to instantly obtain what you need from God. Rather, it is a gift from God that must be coupled with patience as you await the manifestation of God's promises for your life. Hebrews 6:12 instructs, *"Do not become sluggish, but imitate those who through faith and patience inherit the promises."*

The title God has given you in the Bible is not a doubter but a believer. It is only natural for you to function in faith because that is part of your nature as a faith person. In fact, God says His household is one of faith: *"Therefore, as we have opportunity, let us do good to all, especially to those who are of the household of faith"* (Galatians 6:10).

Boldly confess: "I am a faith person. Faith is something I have. God has given me a measure of faith, the spirit of faith. The word of faith is near me, even in my mouth and in my heart, according to Romans 10:8. I declare with John, *'And this is the victory that has overcome the world—our faith'"* (1 John 5:4).

> *Prayer:* Heavenly Father, I thank You for giving me the priceless gift of a measure of faith. Help me to live by faith, never doubting, and to practice patience as I await the fulfillment of Your promises to me. In Jesus's name, amen.
>
> *Thought:* Do you tend to classify yourself as a doubting Thomas or a faith person?
>
> *Readings:* Psalm 11; Hebrews 10:38–39

DAY 45

OWN YOUR FAITH

Don't be a spiritual hitchhiker who depends on others' faith in your times of need. Rather, cultivate your own faith life so that when a crisis occurs, you won't need to ask anyone else to pray the prayer of faith for you; you can do your own praying. If sickness strikes, be ready to be used by God to minister healing to yourself and to others, in Jesus's name.

Remember, "*God has dealt to each one a measure of faith*" (Romans 12:3). Declare it right now: "God has given me a measure of faith. God does not classify me as a doubter, an unbeliever. I am a member of the household of faith. I am a faith person. I say, today and every day, 'Faith is something that I have, for God has given to every Christian a measure of faith.'"

"*Everyone who asks receives, and he who seeks finds, and to him who knocks it will be opened*" (Matthew 7:8)—this is the word of Jesus on the subject. Jesus clearly taught that everyone should do his or her own asking; everyone should do his or her own receiving.

God the Father has no favorites; "*God shows no partiality*" (Acts 10:34). There are no *lucky* people with the Lord. You are just as dear to the Father as any evangelist, pastor, missionary, or teacher. You have just as much righteousness as any other Christian has, for your righteousness is based upon what Jesus has done in your stead. (See 2 Corinthians 5:21.)

As a result of your own, personal faith life, you have access to God twenty-four hours a day, seven days a week, such that you can follow the apostle Paul's admonition to *"pray without ceasing"* (1 Thessalonians 5:17), living a life of *"continuing steadfastly in prayer"* (Romans 12:12). You do not have to look here or there for someone else to pray for you; rather, you can be bold in doing your own praying. You have the right to pray in the name of Jesus to your Father—just as much right as anyone else, for Jesus has said to you, *"Whatever you ask the Father in My name He will give you"* (John 16:23).

Claim your authority as a believer. Cease to be a spiritual hitchhiker and start calling on the name of Jesus at any time of day. The Father loves you just as much as He loves any of His children, so be bold in your faith! Pray to Him, expecting mighty answers. Tell others that you are praying for them. Be a courageous channel of blessing to minister healing and help to those in need. Fearlessly cast out demons in Jesus's name. Dare to speak the Word confidently against all manner of oppression, for you possess faith in the life-giving Word on your lips.

Your faith should be your own. It is the faith of God—your faith in your God.

> *Prayer:* Lord, forgive me for the times when I've been a spiritual hitchhiker. Help me to pray continually, taking full advantage of my access to Your throne. I commit to owning my faith and living boldly by it day by day. In Jesus's name, amen.
>
> *Thought:* When have you demonstrated the traits of a *spiritual hitchhiker?* How can you take ownership of your faith starting today?
>
> *Readings:* Psalm 49; Hebrews 4:14–16

DAY 46

WHAT FAITH IS NOT

"Claiming the promises of God" does not count as faith, because faith counts on already possessing those promises. The act of "claiming" proves that one does not yet have the promise in question. It is unbelief masquerading as faith.

As long as someone is trying to get something, faith has not yet acted. Faith says, "Thank You, Father." Faith has it. Faith has arrived. Faith stops praying and starts praising.

Doubt says, "I claim the promises of God" or "I am standing on the promises of God." These types of statements are the language of doubt.

Unbelief is the state of mind of someone who quotes the Word but does not act upon it. Another term for this kind of approach is *mental assent*.

Some Christians, in the early days of their faith journey, *plead the promises of God* and then claim those promises as theirs. Little do they realize that their very language reveals and reinforces their unbelief.

You see, believing is simply acting on the Word of God. We act on the Word as we would act on the word of a loved one or a trusted friend.

We act on the Word because we know it is true. We don't try to believe it; we don't strive to have faith for it. We don't pray for faith but we simply act on it.

Someone once said, "I am trying to make the Word true." No one needs to do that! The Word has always been true and always will be true.

You cannot know the Word until you begin to practice it and let it live in you. Even if you have been listening to the finest preachers and studying the Bible diligently for years, it is possible that you have never really made the Word part of your life.

Making the Word part of your life—using the Word in your daily living—is the secret of faith. When the Word abides in you, it enables God to express Himself through you as you draw on the Vine for wisdom, love, and ability. You are never without adequate resources.

The Word is the Master speaking through you. When you act on the Word, you act in unison with Him. You and He are lifting your load together and enjoying fellowship with one another. You benefit from being filled with His ability and strength.

Can you see how faith is simply acting on the Word? Be done with mental assent and head knowledge, and move on to a place of walking continually with Him, realizing that His ability has become your own.

Prayer: Heavenly Father, I thank You for the blessed ability to live in faith, counting Your promises as already fulfilled. Help me to quit *claiming* Your promises and start seizing them by faith. In Jesus's name, amen.

Thought: Are you living by faith or mere mental assent?

Readings: Isaiah 55:10–11; 1 John 5:9–13

DON'T SAY "I CAN'T" WHEN GOD SAYS "YOU CAN"

Never say "I can't." You won't find that phrase anywhere in the Bible. Speak God's language only. Say what His Word says. Harmonize with heaven by affirming the Scriptures.

Don't say, "I can't receive my healing." Boldly affirm, "I *can* receive my healing, for by His stripes I am healed. I *can* receive my healing because Jesus said in Mark 16:18 that His followers would lay hands on the sick, and they would recover. Hands have been laid upon me; thus, I am recovering."

Don't say, "I can't pay my bills." Rather, boldly declare, "I *can* pay my bills, for my God shall supply all my need according to His riches in glory by Christ Jesus, as it says in Philippians 4:19. I have honored the Lord by paying my tithes and giving offerings in His name, and He says in Malachi 3:10 that He will open heaven's windows and pour overflowing blessings upon me because of my faithful stewardship. I *can* pay my bills, because my God supplies the money to meet my every need."

Don't say, "I just can't get answers to my prayers." This kind of statement expresses an attitude that will close the heavens to your life. Speak out with assurance, "I *can* receive the answers to my prayers, for Jesus said in John 14:13–14 that whatsoever I ask the Father in His name, that will He give to me. I can receive mighty

Don't Say "I Can't" When God Says "You Can" 127

answers from God, for He has promised in Jeremiah 33:3 that He will answer me and show me great and mighty things when I call to Him. I *can* receive answers to my prayers because I am confident that I have what I ask of Him, since I keep His commandments and do those things that are pleasing in His sight." (See 1 John 3:22.)

Don't say, "I can't see my loved ones coming to salvation in Jesus Christ." Such thinking is a lie of the devil, and for you to speak it would be to give place to the devil. Agree with God's promise and declare, "I *can* see my loved ones coming to salvation in Jesus Christ, for God has promised that if I believe on the Lord Jesus Christ, not only would I be saved, but also, because of my belief, my household shall also be saved. I shall never fear my loved ones' being lost forever in hell. I can see all my loved ones saved because I am God's instrument to believe for their salvation."

Don't say, "I can't overcome my unhealthy habits and lose any weight." Discover the limitless ability of Christ by saying, "I *can* resist eating excessive amounts of rich, fattening foods. Through the indwelling of Christ, I can practice self-restraint and avoid too many high-calorie foods. I *can*, by God's grace, overcome the inclination to be a compulsive eater and instead practice moderation and temperance, for my belly shall not be my god. Hallelujah, I have found the secret: I can conquer my condition through Jesus Christ who is my strength and my sufficiency."

> *Prayer:* Lord, thank You for giving me unlimited ability through Your Word. I commit to speaking only what You have said and not giving place to idle fears and doubts. In Jesus's name, amen.
>
> *Thought:* What negative thoughts have you been entertaining lately? How can you dispel them with the Word of God?
>
> *Readings:* Jeremiah 33; Acts 16:25–34

DAY 48

FEAR HAS NO PART IN YOUR HEART

An astounding number of people from all walks of life are obsessed by some inner fear. However, as a servant of God, you can boldly declare that you *can* be free from fear. Just what is fear? Fear has been defined as the expectation or apprehension of evil.

Within limits, fear can be a healthy thing. We cannot live either our natural or our spiritual lives without it. A child will burn himself unless he or she develops a proper fear of fire. A pedestrian will be knocked down and perhaps killed without a respectful fear of vehicular traffic. And believers cannot be successful in their walk with Christ unless they respectfully fear and reverence God, for *"the fear of the LORD is the beginning of knowledge"* (Proverbs 1:7). It is healthy to fear both danger and sin.

But there is a different sort of fear that is not healthy at all, and this is the fear that brings torment. (See 1 John 4:18.) This kind of fear causes people to expect the worst. It is an insidious monster that, if given free rein in your life, will wreak havoc through misery, defeat, bondage, and destruction.

Satan wants to inflict believers with the diabolical spirit of fear—a spirit that expects and magnifies evil, failure, sickness, danger, and worries. Many people fail to recognize fear when it poses as prudence, caution, or discretion. The devil will use every subtle device that he can find to hinder the good things of God. Fear is the greatest spiritual hindrance keeping people from yielding themselves completely to God and enjoying a rich, abundant life in Christ Jesus.

As we look into God's Word, we find full assurance that we can live free from fear, for fear has no part in the heart of a redeemed child of God. One scriptural guarantee is Isaiah 41:10: *"Fear not, for I am with you; be not dismayed, for I am your God. I will strengthen you, yes, I will help you, I will uphold you with My righteous right hand."* As long as God is with you, fear need have no part in your heart.

God says to you, *"Fear not, for I have redeemed you; I have called you by your name; you are Mine"* (Isaiah 43:1). Because the Lord has redeemed you, you are delivered from the power of Satan, the author of fear.

The next time you feel afraid, challenge yourself to resist your fear. As it says in James 4:7, *"Resist the devil and he will flee from you."* Affirm these Scriptures instead:

> *The LORD is on my side; I will not fear. What can man do to me?* (Psalm 118:6)
>
> *The fear of man brings a snare, but whoever trusts in the LORD shall be safe.* (Proverbs 29:25)

Because God is your unfailing Helper, you can boldly say, "Fear has no part in my heart!"

Prayer: Heavenly Father, I confess that fear has no part in my heart, for You have not given me a spirit of fear but Your power, Your love, and a sound mind. Help me to stand courageously in the face of all my fears, confident that You will give me the victory and will deliver me. In Jesus's name, amen.

Thought: What fears have been plaguing you that you can overcome by your confidence in the mighty presence of God?

Readings: Psalm 27:1–3; Philippians 4:6–7

DAY 49

POWER IN PRAYER

Plenty of people pray, but do they see results? Simply talking into the air is not prayer. We should pray for results. If we pray and nothing follows, we should seek to discover the source of the trouble. The big things of our faith are all supernatural, and if we have no supernatural results to show for our prayers, then the reason must be that we have only the form of godliness and not the power. (See 2 Timothy 3:5.)

Why not get down to first principles and find out what is the matter? Is God untrue? Is the day of praying over? Have the promises we find in the Bible been made by a bankrupt God? It may be that we are not recognized in the bank of heaven. We had better get Jesus to introduce us there!

Jesus has given us the right of attorney to use His name in our prayers to the Father. His words are final: "Whatever you ask the Father in My name He will give you" (John 16:23). We know that Jesus and His Father entered into a wonderful blood covenant with us, and this fact alone guarantees us answers to our prayers.

Next, Jesus gave us the Great Commission and promised to be with us until the end of the age. (See Matthew 28:18–20.) If He sends us out, He will back us up, for no soldier goes out under his own orders. Jesus must answer our prayers and meet our needs.

Speaking of needs, we are faced with many on every side. All around us, people are dying for need of Christ. The sick need healing, and the weak need strength. Are you in God's will? Are you doing the "*good works, which God prepared beforehand that* [you] *should walk in them*" (Ephesians 2:10)? Do you have right standing with the Lord? If your heart condemns you, get down before the mighty One and believe your way through the hosts of demons who would hinder your prayers.

Pray through to victory. If you are praying for the sick, stick to it and don't give up. If you are praying for financial resources, command them to be loosed in the mighty name of Jesus. If you are praying for the salvation of souls, stand by until you see the answer.

Prayer: Lord, forgive me for praying idle prayers and not expecting to receive an answer or to see results. Give me faith and expectation as I lay my requests before You, and show me when I need to mend my relationship with You, that my prayers may not be hindered. In Jesus's name, amen.

Thought: What needs can you take to the Lord in bold, expectant prayer today?

Readings: 2 Chronicles 7:14; John 14:12–14

DAY 50

GUARD YOUR
CONVERSATIONS

Few people truly understand the effect that their conversations have on their own spirits. When you pretend to be what you are not, and you talk glibly about it, your spirit is compromised. It is like a piece of rot in the wooden beam of a structure that weakens the entire building.

Or, perhaps your conversation is full of discouragement, and you constantly talk about your failures and inferiority. If such an attitude pervades your speech, you will find it difficult to rise above that attitude in your heart and mind.

On the other hand, if you speak the truth about who you are in Christ—confessing to your friends and your enemies alike what God is to you, and the fact that you are united to Him; confessing that you are partners with God, and that He is the One who backs you up and furnishes the capital for your endeavors; giving Him credit for His ability and wisdom; daring to boldly confess your expectation of success because of His grace—you will build your faith and preserve the integrity of your belief.

The continual, bold confession of Jesus is our example. We are what He has made us to be. Jesus confessed what He was; likewise, we are to confess what we are in Christ. Those who prize head knowledge and human sense will not understand us. To confess that you are redeemed, that your redemption is an undeniable reality, that you are delivered out of Satan's dominion and authority—that is a daring confession to make. To confess that you are a new creation in Christ Jesus, a partaker of the very nature and life of Deity, might amaze your friends. It isn't confessing these truths once that counts but daily affirming your relationship to God, claiming your righteousness, and testifying to your ability to stand in His presence without any sense of guilt or inferiority.

You see, there are two kinds of truth—sense knowledge truth and revelation truth—and they are usually opposed to each other. Live in the new realm, above the senses, so you hold fast to your confession that you are what God's Word says you are.

Dare to stand in the presence of sense knowledge and widely recognized "facts." For instance, sense knowledge may declare that you are sick with an incurable disease. If that is the case, you should confess that God laid that disease on Jesus, and that by His stripes you are healed. You are to hold fast your confession in the face of any apparent contradictions from the natural world. Sense knowledge will say that you are confessing an untruth, but you will be confessing what God says.

Or suppose your senses indicate that you are in dire financial need. The Word declares, *"My God shall supply all your need"* (Philippians 4:19), and so you must call God's attention to the information from your senses and also to what you expect, by faith, that He will do for you. Because you know that He who is within you is greater than the forces that surround you, including your senses, you can maintain your confession of spiritual truth in the face of sensory contradictions.

> **Prayer:** Father God, I proclaim that You are more than enough for all my needs. Help me to maintain my positive confession in spite of any contradictory sense knowledge. In Jesus's name, amen.
>
> **Thought:** Do you tend to pay more attention to sense knowledge or revelation truth?
>
> **Readings:** Ecclesiastes 10:11–12; 1 John 4:1–6

DAY 51

AVOID RECKLESS WORDS AND ANGRY OUTBURSTS

A famous preacher once lost his temper. As a result, he damaged his influence on an unsaved man who was interested in salvation.

As Christian believers, we must always be on guard lest we bring dishonor to the gospel by losing our temper or being careless with our words. *"One who is slow to anger is better than the mighty, and one whose temper is controlled than one who captures a city"* (Proverbs 16:32 NRSV).

Some people pride themselves on their quick tempers and witty retorts, but God calls it a virtue to be slow to anger. His Word cautions us, *"Do not hasten in your spirit to be angry, for anger rests in the bosom of fools"* (Ecclesiastes 7:9).

Now, if you find that you tend to anger quickly and are prone to outbursts of rage, it could be a factor of your not having been born again—not yet being regenerated. You can obtain salvation today by repenting of your sins and by believing in your heart and confessing with your mouth that the Lord Jesus Christ died on the cross for your sins and then rose again so that you might live forever. (See Romans 10:9.)

Or, it could be that you are already born again but have not been baptized in the Holy Spirit. This, too, can be taken care of as you read God's Word and accept His promise for yourself. (See Acts 2:38–39.)

If you are already a Christian believer, don't attempt to justify your wrong spirit. Some people try to explain away their tempers, by saying, "Oh, that's just my Irish blood," or "That's the German in me." However, if we are new creatures in Christ, and we are truly walking in the Spirit, then old things have passed away, and every part of us has become new. (See 2 Corinthians 5:17.)

Psalm 37:8 gives the following command: *"Cease from anger, and forsake wrath; do not fret—it only causes harm."* God says to us, *"Cease from anger."* We are to put anger and its rash, reckless manifestations away from our lives. As Paul instructs us in Colossians 3:8, *"Put off all these: anger, wrath, malice, blasphemy, filthy language out of your mouth."*

Replacing that anger, we are to let God cultivate the fruit of the Spirit in our hearts. *"The fruit of the Spirit is love, joy, peace, longsuffering, kindness, goodness, faithfulness, gentleness, self-control"* (Galatians 5:22–23).

Boldly overcome your anger, for God says, *"He who overcomes shall inherit all things, and I will be his God and he shall be My son"* (Revelation 21:7).

Prayer: Father God, by the power of Your Spirit, purify my heart from anger and its ugly manifestations through words and deeds. Create in me a clean heart that produces the fruit of Your Spirit and leads to a life that glorifies You. In Jesus's name, amen.

Thought: Have you allowed a spirit of anger to persist in your heart, justifying its presence and explaining it away? If so, repent today and seek a renewed spirit that is not governed by anger or malice.

Readings: Psalm 37; Ephesians 4:25–32

DAY 52

ACTING ON THE WORD

James wrote, *"Be doers of the word, and not hearers only, deceiving yourselves"* (James 1:22). A *"doer"* of the Word is one who lives the Word. The Word is at work in you to the measure that you live it out. You live in the Word to the measure that the Word functions in your day-to-day life.

Jesus said we are to abide in Him as He abides in us. (See John 15:7.) Given this reality, your prayers can be very simple. Why? Because the Word on your lips will be God's Word. God will use your lips to speak back to Himself. Through your lips, God can ask what He will, and it will be given to you.

God's Word becomes a living thing on your lips, just as it was a living thing on the lips of Jesus during His earthly ministry. At the tomb of Lazarus, Jesus prayed, *"Father, I thank You that You have heard Me. And I know that You always hear Me"* (John 11:41–42). When the Word abides in you as it lives in Jesus, you can say the very same thing to the Father.

When you accepted Christ into your heart, you received eternal life, being brought into the family of God as a son or daughter. Now, it's time to act like a child of God! Take your place and assume your God-given responsibilities. You don't have to *try* to be a child of God; you already *are* one. You don't have to try to get more faith, because all things belong to you, as a member of God's family.

You should continue to grow in intimacy with the Father through Jesus, and you can do this in a number of ways. Reading the Gospels is one way. Studying the whole of the Scriptures, especially the writings of Paul, is another way. Prayer is, of course, a great way of knowing Him, too. But you really get to know God when you start putting His Word into practice.

When you become a "*doer*" of the Word—when you pray with those who are sick, when you learn to discredit earthly "wisdom" that contradicts the truth, when you study the Bible as if it were the Father's current message to you—then you will know Him.

Talk with your heavenly Father. Fellowship with Him as you would with a loved one living under your roof. Then you will know the Father and will live out His Word in a powerful way.

Prayer: Father God, I thank You for the incredible gift of fellowship with You. Help me to draw ever closer to You through Bible study, through prayer, and especially through the living out of Your Word. In Jesus's name, amen.

Thought: What practices have you been using to draw closer to your heavenly Father?

Readings: Isaiah 43:1; James 1:22–25

DAY 53

BEING LED BY GOD

Because we are the *sheep* in the flock of Jesus, the Good Shepherd, we can and should expect to receive guidance from Him. Jesus Himself said, *"My sheep hear My voice, and I know them, and they follow Me"* (John 10:27).

The Scriptures provide plenty of exhortations to heed the guidance of God as we go about our days and plan out our lives. Consider the following examples:

> *A man's heart plans his way, but the LORD directs his steps.*
> (Proverbs 16:9)
>
> *There are many plans in a man's heart, nevertheless the LORD's counsel—that will stand.* (Proverbs 19:21)
>
> *Trust in the LORD with all your heart, and lean not on your own understanding; in all your ways acknowledge Him, and He shall direct your paths.* (Proverbs 3:5–6)
>
> *Your word is a lamp to my feet and a light to my path.*
> (Psalm 119:105)

We should not make guidance complicated. One thing we can be sure of is that any guidance that we receive from God must be in harmony with His Word and never contradictory to it. The Holy Spirit always uses the Word, for *"the sword of the Spirit…is the word of God"* (Ephesians 6:17).

The Holy Spirit would never lead a Christian believer to marry an unbeliever, for example, because that would be a violation of

God's Word, which tells us, *"Do not be unequally yoked together with unbelievers"* (2 Corinthians 6:14).

Nor would the Holy Spirit lead a true Christian to walk in darkness. As Jesus said, *"I am the light of the world. He who follows Me shall not walk in darkness"* (John 8:12).

In all things, submit to the lordship of your heavenly Father. Confess today: "Jesus is Lord; I trust Him with all my heart."

Give God the freedom to speak to you in the way He chooses. Pray as Samuel did: *"Speak, for your servant is listening"* (1 Samuel 3:10 NRSV). God may choose to speak with an audible voice (see, for example, Exodus 3:4–5), through dreams (see, for example, Matthew 2:13), or through visions (see, for example, Isaiah 6). One of the most common manners in which God gives guidance is revealed in Isaiah 30:21: *"Your ears shall hear a word behind you, saying, 'This is the way, walk in it,' whenever you turn to the right hand or whenever you turn to the left."*

Seek God's leading, and realize that the Lord may use other people to confirm the guidance you receive. At the same time, beware of counterfeit guidance from those with ulterior motives. *"Do not believe every spirit, but test the spirits, whether they are of God; because many false prophets have gone out into the world"* (1 John 4:1).

Prayer: Heavenly Father, thank You for the privilege of receiving guidance from Your Holy Spirit. Help me to submit to Your ways and to seek Your leading in every aspect of my life. In Jesus's name, amen.

Thought: Do you seek and submit to the Lord's guidance in all matters?

Readings: Psalm 25; John 16:5–15

DAY 54

GOD'S CURE FOR
YOUR CARES

The Bible is a book full of cures for diseases of all kinds. The salvation Jesus purchased for us provides a cure for every condition the devil could possibly lay on you, whether diseases of the spirit or ailments of the body.

Many spiritual diseases, if not cured early on, can lead to physical illness. The following are some examples of spiritual diseases and the scriptural prescription for their cure.

Worry. Jesus asked, *"Which of you by worrying can add one cubit to his stature?"* (Matthew 6:27). In other words, what will you gain by worrying? Jesus also said, *"Do not worry about your life, what you will eat or what you will drink; nor about your body, what you will put on. Is not life more than food and the body more than clothing?"* (verse 25). He went on to give the sure cure for worry: *"Seek first the kingdom of God and His righteousness, and all these things shall be added to you"* (verse 33). When your heart is fixed on the things of the Spirit, you can have confidence that God will meet your every need.

Guilt. Are you burdened with feelings of guilt? If your life is filled with sin and your heart is not right with God, there is a cure: *"The blood of Jesus Christ His Son cleanses us from all sin....If we confess our sins, He is faithful and just to forgive us our sins and to cleanse us from all unrighteousness"* (1 John 1:7, 9). Confess your sins and accept Christ's forgiveness. Then you can live free from the condemnation and guilt of sin.

Nervousness. Few things hinder our ability to enjoy life to the fullest more than anxiety. If you are prone to fretting, read Psalm 91 in its entirety. This magnificent psalm begins, *"He who dwells in the secret place of the Most High shall abide under the shadow of the Almighty"* (verse 1). When you make a habit of dwelling in the secret place—in the presence of God—you will be filled with His perfect joy, so that you will be able to echo the psalmist in saying, *"In Your presence is fullness of joy; at Your right hand are pleasures forevermore"* (Psalm 16:11).

Insomnia. Are you plagued with sleeplessness? Let me prescribe the following verses: *"I will both lie down in peace, and sleep; for You alone, O LORD, make me dwell in safety"* (Psalm 4:8) and *"He gives His beloved sleep"* (Psalm 127:2). Lie down and, in the name of Jesus, go to sleep, enjoying the rest that God has provided for you.

The "blues." Have you ever felt a spirit of depression and despondency that grips you in a way that weighs on your heart? The next time you find yourself feeling this way, proclaim Psalm 42:5: *"Why are you cast down, O my soul? And why are you disquieted within me? Hope in God, for I shall yet praise Him for the help of His countenance."* A sure cure for a case of the blues is to sing God's praises.

God has the cure for all your cares. Nothing can cheat you out of His blessings, His healing, and His deliverance if you will believe and obey His Word.

Prayer: Heavenly Father, I praise You for providing the cure for my every ailment. Help me to take refuge in Your Word and experience the fullness of Your promises to heal, deliver, and give me a joy that surpasses all circum-stances. In Jesus's name, amen.

Thought: What ailments will you seek God's cure for today?

Readings: Psalm 91; Matthew 11:28–30

DAY 55

BEING MIRACLE-MINDED

Are miracles part of God's plan for us today? The church began with miracles. Healing the sick is miraculous. So is walking on water. But when God imparts His nature to a man such as Saul of Tarsus, whose hands were wet with the blood of Christian believers he had slain, and in a single moment makes him a new creation, that is the miracle of all miracles.

Christianity is a miracle—God's intrusion into the human realm, the Spirit's prevailing over physical forces. A miracle is God's way of restoring what Satan has destroyed. Jesus Himself was a miracle. His incarnation was a miracle. The senses cannot understand these things, for they belong to the spiritual realm.

If you take the miraculous out of Christianity, you are left with nothing but philosophy, and philosophy provides only sensory knowledge that is powerless to transform people. Yet the world today has become more doubt-minded than miracle-minded. In academia, it is a mark of scholarship to put a question mark at the end of every sentence and challenge all the old landmarks.

Doubt has never signified strength. It isn't doubting something but believing something that makes a person strong. Doubts bring unhealthy reactions, while faith always produces healthy reactions.

Blessed is the person who is faith-minded toward God and toward the Bible, who reaches a place where faith is cultivated and doubts are unwanted. The next step beyond that is becoming miracle-minded. Jesus was miracle-minded. Elijah was miracle-minded. Paul and Peter were miracle-minded. Once someone becomes miracle-minded, you will start seeing events that characterized the apostolic church. But among doubt-minded people, nothing miraculous occurs.

Miracle-mindedness comes from a close walk with the Lord Jesus. You see, the further we go from the Master, the dimmer our faith becomes. The nearer we get to Him, the more clearly we see Him with eyes of faith. If you are dominated by doubt, you are a long way from the Master. If you are dominated by faith, you are walking closely with Him.

Ask the Lord to help you to live in the realm of the Word, in the realm of faith, so that you grow into a miracle-minded person. The rest of the world lives in the realm of reason, and you can't live in the realm of reason and please God.

You were given the faculty of reasoning in order that it might be sanctified by the Spirit and brought into captivity by the Lord Jesus (see 2 Corinthians 10:5) so you can think God's thoughts after Him. It was not given to you to cultivate doubt, fear, or skepticism, or to rebel against God's Word and the mind of Christ.

Prayer: Almighty God, I commit to cultivating my faith and putting an end to my doubts. I will be a faith-minded individual and a miracle-minded believer, welcoming Your miraculous ways and believing rather than doubting. In Jesus's name, amen.

Thought: Have you tended to live more in the realm of reason or the realm of faith?

Readings: Isaiah 55:8–9; 2 Corinthians 5:3–6

DAY 56

LIVING A
SUPERNATURAL LIFE

Supernatural—the very word breathes of miracles. Christianity itself is supernatural. It is the union of deity and humanity, a union that was first manifested in the Man of Galilee, then appeared again on the day of Pentecost, when 120 men and women were united with the Holy Spirit. (See Acts 2:1–4.)

The new birth is supernatural—a miraculous partaking of the nature of God. Every child of God is a miracle. When the Spirit of God comes into a person's body and makes it His home, a miracle has taken place. That person is now capable of living in the Spirit realm, where Jesus lived when He was on earth.

The faith realm, the love realm, and the Spirit realm represent the place where we meet God. The person who walks by faith and not by reason is walking in the supernatural. The person who walks in love lives in the realm that is higher than reason. That's supernatural.

It is the nature of humankind to be selfish, but the miraculous love of Jesus takes us out of the realm of selfishness and into the realm of God. The person who walks in the Spirit is walking in the realm above reason or physical evidences. He or she may experience those things but does not exist in their realm.

When the Lord said, *"Fear not, for I am with you; be not dismayed, for I am your God. I will strengthen you, yes, I will help you, I will uphold you with My righteous right hand"* (Isaiah 41:10), He was actually participating in the daily activities of His children. He was being a partner with us in all that we are and do.

In a supernatural fashion, God makes us one with Himself. He gives us His strength so that it becomes our own. His life becomes our life. His wisdom and love become ours. We are utterly identified with Him. He becomes a part of all we do, so that we can surely say, *"I can do all things through Christ who strengthens me"* (Philippians 4:13).

God supernaturally takes us out of the realm of weakness, fear, and inability, and moves us into the realm of His own limitless ability. We become supermen and superwomen! By His grace, we know that *"He who is in* [us] *is greater than he who is in the world"* (1 John 4:4). Because of this confidence, we may fearlessly undertake the impossible.

No longer do we count on our weaknesses, our limitations, our lack of knowledge, or our scarcity of resources. We count on the One who has called us into fellowship with His Son Jesus Christ as we live a supernatural life!

Prayer: Father God, thank You for giving me Your own wholeness, wisdom, power, and love. I no longer count on my own weaknesses but stand on Your strength. Empower me to live a supernatural life, to Your glory and praise. In Jesus's name, amen.

Thought: In what ways have you witnessed the supernatural ways of God overruling your selfish, fleshly desires?

Readings: Isaiah 40:10–31; 1 John 4:1–16

DAY 57

BOLD GIVING

The most joyful Christians are those who know the blessing of bold giving. When you give boldly and generously, you have God's permission to affirm, "I am proving my God. He is pouring out an overflowing blessing for me. He is rebuking the devourer for my sake!" (See Malachi 3:11.)

The Bible says that when we give, we honor the Lord. The result is God's promise that He will reward us with plenty:

> Honor the LORD with your possessions, and with the first-fruits of all your increase; so your barns will be filled with plenty, and your vats will overflow with new wine.
>
> (Proverbs 3:9–10)

The blessing for giving boldly is that it opens the windows of heaven (see Malachi 3:10), and its reward is *given to you: good measure, pressed down, shaken together, and running over*" (Luke 6:38). Your spiritual and material reward for bold giving is plenty. On top of this, your bold giving sends forth the gospel for the winning of souls and the meeting of needs.

Dare to abandon yourself to God's promises in your giving. You will not only "*lay up...treasures in heaven*" (Matthew 6:20), but you will also experience tremendous joy in the here and now.

You will find yourself receiving abundantly in return for your giving, for only givers are receivers. Only as you give do you have the capacity to receive. This is the law of love in action.

Giving and receiving are so closely allied throughout the Old and New Testaments that it behooves all children of God to keep a careful watch on their giving—the giving of money, the giving of tithes, the giving of love, the giving of time, and the giving of the Word.

We could offer you many illustrations of people who prayed for healing and failed to receive it until they started tithing faithfully. There would be more giving if everyone truly understood the blessings that come through it. Money is the smallest part of real giving—a friendly word or taking time to shake hands with someone or smile at them is also a gift to others.

And think of the gift of prayers! We must say gently to our brothers and sisters, "I am praying for you. I was interceding on your behalf before the Lord this morning." As it is, we do not bear other people's burdens as we ought. We do not carry loads as we should. It is easy to give a dollar, but to give our time, love, and wisdom is to be blessed.

Jesus said, *"Freely have you received, freely give"* (Matthew 10:8). To us, He says, "I have given Myself to you with utter abandon. Now, I want you to give yourselves to others with utter abandon. I want you to give your whole being to the church and to the world."

What a challenge this is! And yet *"he who sows sparingly will also reap sparingly, and he who sows bountifully will also reap bountifully"* (2 Corinthians 9:6). Do you desire a large harvest? Then give! Will not a large acreage yield a large harvest? You will give of your best if you want to get God's best.

Prayer: Father God, I thank You for richly blessing me, that I might be a blessing to others. Help me to give bountifully of my resources, time, and love so that others may benefit and that You may be glorified. In Jesus's name, amen.

Thought: What kind of a harvest are you sowing today?

Readings: Malachi 3:8–12; 2 Corinthians 9:6–15

DAY 58

BOLD LOVE

Love *"does not seek its own"* (1 Corinthians 13:5). That is the law of love. Selfishness always seeks its own, but love lives for others, because that is what Jesus did. As the very embodiment of love, *"He died for all, that those who live should live no longer for themselves, but for Him who died for them and rose again"* (2 Corinthians 5:15).

Jesus lived in His Father's love and kept His Father's Word. His commandment to us is that we follow in His footsteps by loving one another, bearing one another's infirmities and burdens. (See John 13:34; Romans 15:1–3; Galatians 6:2.)

First Peter gives us a picture of walking in the steps of the Master. Read this passage over and over again until it becomes a part of your life:

> To this you were called, because Christ also suffered for us, leaving us an example, that you should follow His steps: "Who committed no sin, nor was deceit found in His mouth"; who, when He was reviled, did not revile in return; when He suffered, He did not threaten, but committed Himself to Him who judges righteously; who Himself bore our sins in His own body on the tree, that we, having died to sins, might live for righteousness—by whose stripes you were healed.
>
> (1 Peter 2:21–24)

Next, turn to Ephesians 5:1–2: *"Be imitators of God as dear children. And walk in love."* The person who continually walks in love will never sin, for sin is stepping out of love. And as you walk in love, you walk in the light of God's Word, with a continual sense of God's protection and care. You walk in the Lord, and that walk will never let you act selfishly or be unkind or bitter; it will lead you to be just like the Master, so that you can say with the psalmist, *"The* Lord *is my light and my salvation; whom shall I fear? The* Lord *is the strength of my life; of whom shall I be afraid?"* (Psalm 27:1).

As long as you walk in love, you are in the light, and you will not stumble; you will be able to rest confidently in the Word that says, *"Fear not, for I am with you"* (Isaiah 41:10). God is with you; God is in you. God is the strength of your life. You cannot be sick. You cannot be weak. You cannot be ignorant of His will. You know what His mind is, because He is imparting Himself and His ability to you.

He will enable you to show love and kindness to others, *"tenderhearted, forgiving one another, even as God in Christ forgave you"* (Ephesians 4:32). He will enable you to be patient with young people and understanding of the impetuousness of youth. He will enable you to show kindness to the elderly and to sympathize with those in the hospital by visiting them and expressing your concern. You can show kindness to those behind prison bars, fulfilling Jesus's command to visit prisoners. (See Matthew 25:36.)

The bold love of Christ dwelling within you will enable you to be kind and sympathetic toward others, gracious and friendly, benevolent toward the less privileged, and congenial in all your relationships.

Prayer: Heavenly Father, I praise You for Your love and for filling me with it. I declare today that I am walking in Your love and in Your light, and that my actions toward others will be benevolent, charitable, and selfless. May my life be a testament to Your great love. In Jesus's name, amen.

Thought: Who are the "least of these" to whom you can show God's love today?

Readings: Jeremiah 31:3; 1 Corinthians 13

DAY 59

BOLD SINGING

We find great victory in singing praises to the Lord. There is a real release and therapy in singing songs of spiritual liberation, songs of testimony, and songs about the Lord's power and keeping. *"Let the saints be joyful in glory; let them sing aloud on their beds. Let the high praises of God be in their mouth, and a two-edged sword in their hand"* (Psalm 149:5–6). It is real, bold Bible living to cultivate a singing heart!

Heartfelt singing is charged with divine power. There are two primary secrets to maintaining a singing heart: being full of the Word and being full of the Spirit.

Colossians 3:16 says, *"Let the word of Christ dwell in you richly in all wisdom, teaching and admonishing one another in psalms and hymns and spiritual songs, singing with grace in your hearts to the Lord."* When you are full of the Word, it produces a bold, glad song within you. Confessing the Word aloud will bring forth an anthem of praise from your lips. Learn to approach your troubles with song; when griefs arise, sing them down. Praise God with song, and you will be lifted above trials of every sort.

In his letter to the Ephesians, Paul provides the following instructions that describe being full of the Spirit:

Do not be drunk with wine, in which is dissipation; but be filled with the Spirit, speaking to one another in psalms and hymns and spiritual songs, singing and making melody in your heart to the Lord, giving thanks always for all things to

God the Father in the name of our Lord Jesus Christ.
(Ephesians 5:18–20)

When you are controlled by God's Spirit, He invariably inspires much song from your heart.

Every great move of the Spirit throughout history has been characterized by bold, gallant singing. What did the Israelites do when God delivered them from Egypt with a mighty hand? They sang praises to the Lord! (See Exodus 15:1–2.) What was it that produced one of the most unusual divine interventions in the New Testament? Paul and Silas, imprisoned and in chains, were singing and praying in earshot of their fellow prisoners when an earthquake rattled the foundations of the prison and caused the cell doors to be flung open and the chains to be loosed. (See Acts 16:25–26.)

Our circumstances may be dismal at times, and we may feel overwhelmed by troubles, but our difficulties are usually mild compared to those of Paul and Silas when they were imprisoned. However, those two men were the righteous of the Lord, as bold as lions, and they could sing praises to God even under such circumstances. God intervened for them, and He will intervene for us if we exhibit such loving confidence and bold faith in our God, praising Him in song regardless of how defeated we may feel.

There is no defeat to the bold Christian who sings God's praises. God delights in our songs to Him! Whether we have a talent for singing or not, we are singing best when we are singing unto the Lord.

Prayer: Father God, please fill my heart with songs of praise, so that I may conquer my adversaries through the worship that flows from my lips. May I ever sing praises to Your name, thereby triumphing over every circumstance and finding Your joy to be my strength. In Jesus's name, amen.

Thought: The next time you feel beset by troubles, try singing a song of praise to God instead.

Readings: Psalm 100; 1 Corinthians 14:15

DAY 60

A WITNESS TO BLESS THE WORLD

It is when we realize that we will never rise above our confession that we reach a place where God can really start to use us. When we confess His Word and hold fast to that confession, we sow our words and faith into the hearts of those who hear us. Let's make sure that the verbal seeds we sow are the Word of God, as they were in the parable of the sower. (See Luke 8:5–8, 11–15.)

Too many believers sow seeds of fear and doubt by negating their testimony with the way they live or by speaking words of doom and gloom. It is only when we confess the Word of God—declaring emphatically, for example, "By His stripes I am healed" (see Isaiah 53:5)—and hold fast to that confession that we will see our deliverance, thereby producing a witness that can grow the faith of those who hear and see us.

The testimony that we make has the power to overcome the devil. (See Revelation 12:11.) Our words will beget either faith or doubt in the hearts of others, for *"death and life are in the power of the tongue"* (Proverbs 18:21).

Never underestimate the power of your words! God created the universe with faith-filled words. (See Genesis 1.) And most of the sick people whom Jesus healed during His earthly ministry were healed with words. To the woman with the issue of blood who by faith touched the hem of His garment, Jesus said, *"Be of good cheer, daughter; your faith has made you well"* (Matthew 9:22).

To the two blind men who confessed aloud their belief in His ability to heal them, He said, *"According to your faith let it be to you"* (Matthew 9:29).

The words of Jesus even raised the dead to life. To the corpse of Lazarus as it lay in the tomb, He said, *"Lazarus, come forth!"* (John 11:43).

The devil is whipped by the words of Jesus. Our lips can be the means of transportation of God's deliverance from heaven to the needs of people here on earth. We can use God's Word as the powerful tool it is. Whispering or shouting, we can say, "In Jesus's name, demon, come out of him." Jesus has assured us, *"These signs will follow those who believe: In My name they will cast out demons;… they will lay hands on the sick, and they will recover"* (Mark 16:17, 18).

By the example of your confession and the bold pronouncement of God's Word, you can reap a harvest of hearts that believe and bodies that are healed.

> *Prayer:* Lord God, I ask You to use my confession of Your Word to not only grow faith in the hearts of others but also to work healings in their bodies and lives. Allow me to do the things that Jesus did. In His name, amen.
>
> *Thought:* Who can you bless today with your testimony and your bold proclamation of God's Word?
>
> *Readings:* Proverbs 18; Mark 16:15–18

ABOUT THE AUTHORS

D r. E. W. Kenyon (1867–1948) was born in Saratoga County, New York. At age nineteen, he preached his first sermon. He pastored several churches in New England and founded the Bethel Bible Institute in Spencer, Massachusetts. This school later became the Providence Bible Institute when it was relocated to Providence, Rhode Island.

Kenyon served as an evangelist for over twenty years. In 1931, he became a pioneer in Christian radio on the Pacific Coast with his show *Kenyon's Church of the Air*, for which he earned the moniker "The Faith Builder." He also began the New Covenant Baptist Church in Seattle.

In addition to his pastoral and radio ministries, Kenyon wrote extensively. Among his books are the Bible courses *The Bible in the Light of Our Redemption: From Genesis Through Revelation* and *Studies in the Deeper Life: A Scriptural Study of Great Christian Truths*, and more than twenty other works, including *The Wonderful Name of Jesus, Two Kinds of Faith, In His Presence: The Secret of Prayer, The Blood Covenant, The Hidden Man, Jesus the Healer, New Creation Realities*, and *Two Kinds of Righteousness*.

D on Gossett (1929–2014) served the Lord in active ministry for more than sixty years as pastor, worldwide evangelist, missionary, and longtime broadcaster. Born again at age twelve, Don answered his call to the ministry just five years later and began by reaching out to his unsaved family members. He apprenticed with many well-known evangelists, including William Freeman, Raymond T. Richey, Jack Coe, and T. L. Osborn.

Don's acclaimed daily radio broadcast, *Bold Bible Living*, began in 1961 and was heard in eighty-nine nations over the years. As a missionary evangelist, he personally ministered in sixty-five nations with signs and wonders following the Word of God.

Don authored several bestselling books, including *What You Say Is What You Get*, *There's Dynamite in Praise*, *Living Without Fear*, and *I'm Sold on Being Bold*. His writings have been translated into eighteen languages, with more than 25 million copies in print.